Playing Software

Playing Software

Homo Ludens in Computational Culture

Miguel Sicart

The MIT Press
Cambridge, Massachusetts | London, England

The MIT Press would like to thank the anonymous peer reviewers who provided comments on drafts of this book. The generous work of academic experts is essential for establishing the authority and quality of our publications. We acknowledge with gratitude the contributions of these otherwise uncredited readers.

This book was set in Stone Serif and Stone Sans by Westchester Publishing Services. Printed and bound in the United States of America.

Library of Congress Cataloging-in-Publication Data

Names: Sicart, Miguel, 1978– author.
Title: Playing software : homo ludens in computational culture / Miguel Sicart.
Description: Cambridge, Massachusetts ; London, England : The MIT Press, 2023. | Includes bibliographical references and index.
Identifiers: LCCN 2022011635 (print) | LCCN 2022011636 (ebook) | ISBN 9780262047722 (Hardcover) | ISBN 9780262373173 (epub) | ISBN 9780262373180 (pdf)
Subjects: LCSH: Play. | Human -computer interaction. | Electronic games. | Role playing. | Mass media and culture. | Information technology—Moral and ethical aspects. | Information technology—Economic aspects.
Classification: LCC GV14 .S5193 2023 (print) | LCC GV14 (ebook) | DDC 794.8/1—dc23/eng/20220908
LC record available at https://lccn.loc.gov/2022011635
LC ebook record available at https://lccn.loc.gov/2022011636

10 9 8 7 6 5 4 3 2 1

Contents

Preface

I thought I was done writing about play, and look where I am: writing the acknowledgments and preface for another book about play. The worst part is that I still think it is fun writing whole books about play.

The process is fun first and foremost because of the great folks at the MIT Press. I especially thank Noah Springer for getting this project to the finish line. Thanks also to Lillian Dunaj for patiently dealing with all the processes toward publication. This book is especially indebted to its first editor, Doug Sery, who believed in it and helped shape its early versions, turning my ramblings into a table of contents, a book proposal, and sample chapters. Thanks for everything, Doug—this one is for you.

I like to think about this book as my California project. Thanks to the efforts of my then boss, Laura Beloff, I was awarded a sabbatical that I decided to spend with the wonderful playful people at UC Santa Cruz. Thanks to Michael Mateas, Katherine Isbister, Michael John, Jim Whitehead, Noah Wardrip-Fruin, Arnav Jhala, Soraya Murray, and Susana Ruiz for welcoming me and giving me the time and space to think about all the crazy stuff in this book. In California I learned to appreciate fun in a different way. I also thank the forever friends we made there: Patrick Chuang, Steve McKay, and Amy Keys.

This book was first presented in its current form at a workshop at RMIT University. Thanks to Larissa Hjorth for inviting me and giving me license to talk about whatever I wanted for three days (a dangerous thing to encourage me to do!).

I am privileged to work at the Center for Computer Games Research, surrounded by colleagues and students from whom I learn anew the value of play. Special thanks to Martin Pichlmair and Hajo Backe—friends of shared tastes whom I can always trust will call it when what I say makes no sense and I am just hand waving. My students in the courses Playable Media and PlayLab have been instrumental in refining my ideas so that they were somewhat comprehensible outside my own head. I owe them many sanity points.

Many thanks to the artists Ben Grosser, Pippin Barr, Caroline Sinders, Cade Diehm, and Kyle McDonald for the image rights to their work.

While writing this book was fun, making and publishing ridiculous software is probably the most entertaining thing I've done in my career, and I'm happy that some of it has ended up in this book. Thanks to Irina Shklovski and Christina Neumayer for aiding and abetting each single stupid idea I had about "an app I want to make." And thanks to Luca Rossi for not stopping us!

Ane and Carlos and Silas make everything fun—thank you.

I have written books and articles and given talks and keynotes, but I still think that my most important contributions happen in the daily engagement with students. I would like to also dedicate this book to the two teachers from whom I learned the most about being a teacher, so many years ago: to Teresa Moure, for all the revolutions, and to Francisco Mateo, who started it all.

I have tried to do something a bit different with this book. For example, there are academic references and a reading list, but the mode of argumentation is not always classically academic. This is an academic book, don't get me wrong, but I hope that it is one of a different kind. There is some close analysis of phenomena, but I preferred to give a broad overview rather than a detailed analysis. My goal is to write a book of ideas—a collection of connected thoughts that I hope will spark conversations, discussions, disagreements, and revolts.

The ideas that I present here are based on conventional, classic academic research, and for readers who are interested in those depths, here's the list of my peer-reviewed published articles where I presented the main thesis of the book:

"Quixotean Play in the Age of Computation." *American Journal of Play* 10, no. 3 (2018): 249–264.

"Play in the Information Age." *Philosophy and Technology* 32 (2019): 517–539.

"Playing Software: The Role of The Ludic in the Software Society." *Information, Communication, and Society* 23, no. 14 (2020): 2081–2095.

"Playthings." *Games and Culture* 17, no. 1 (2022): 140–155.

"Playful Capitalism, or Play as an Instrument of Capital." *Contracampo* 40, no. 2 (2021): 50103.

"Pataphysical Software: (Ridiculous) Technological Solutions for Imaginary Problems," in *Proceedings of the 2020 ACM Designing Interactive Systems Conference*, 1859–1871 (with Irina Shklovski). New York: ACM, 2020.

But I don't want this to be a book-length article. I don't even want to be *right*. I want to present a set of ideas that I think make sense and let readers play with them. I hope this book opens possibilities and provokes new ideas or heated counterarguments. I hope the way I see this software society we live in is somewhat contagious through these words and that we end up somewhere, together, talking about these and other ideas and having fun.

0
Start

Playing software is a way of making sense of the world in which human and digital artificial agents meet. This book explores that process, rethinking the role and ethos of play in the information age.

Now, that's a lot for a couple of sentences, so let me dig deeper.

This is a book of ideas, an exploration of a series of premises driven by observation and reflection on phenomena, as well as on (modest) interventions. The first premise of the book concerns the time in which it is written: we live in the information age, an era defined by how software affects all facets of human life. Essentially this book is about play in digital societies. The second premise is that in digital societies, play has a role in shaping our understanding and experience of software. From this premise, I draw a first hypothesis: playing software has a fundamental role in creating and shaping the culture of the information age. From new forms of entertainment, such as video games, to instruments for socializing that have elements of play, like social networks, play is ever present in the information age.

The exploration of that hypothesis leads to proposing a series of arguments. First, this book argues that digital play is significantly different from analog play. Digital play is a particular relation established between human and digital artificial agency. This argument is premised on the understanding of software as agent. From this premise, I propose that our way of thinking about and creating digital technology is a consequence of relating to the agency of software. Computer programs do things, that is, they act in the world, and we humans relate to these programs in specific ways. Playing is a form of relating to the agency of software.

A second argument of this book states that by playing, we shape software agency, and our agency becomes shaped by software. To design software is to design a form of agency and the ways it will relate to artificial agency. Similarly, playing is a form of experiencing the agency of software, adapting and relating to it. In doing so, new cultural, social, and political forms emerge.

Exploring these arguments implies explaining the role of play in shaping our relations with software agencies. For that, we need to know what we talk about when we discuss play. Although classic theorists of play, from Johan Huizinga to Roger Caillois and Bernard Suits, could have provided a valuable foundation for this book, I ground my understanding of play in a different tradition altogether. This book extends María Lugones's concept of playfulness as world traveling as a way of understanding playful relations with software. Briefly put, to play is to travel to others' worlds to meet them there. Playing is constructing identities as we meet with others in other worlds. It involves a generous, curious, joyful form of constructing ourselves and meeting others. In this book, I add some elements to this approach to develop the sketch of a theory of digital play as meeting with and relating to software in a world where the computational and the human coexist.

As a consequence of adopting Lugones's theory, this book also provides a framework toward an *ethos* of digital play. In her work, world traveling is "loving," willing to engage, understand, and grow with others. I propose that the ethos of digital play should also be drawn on this understanding of "loving." Playing software can be a form of exploring the pleasures of relating to other agents, human and computational. More specifically, playing software can be about the liberatory fun of playing with and within the rules and boundaries of computational systems, together with software agents. That pleasure, however, can also have a dark side. Playing software can also be instrumentalization of the pleasure of relating to computational agents that reduces human agency to mere input for a cybernetic system of control.

This is the final argument of this book: while playing software can be a liberating and joyful exploration of the mutual agencies of humans and software, and the way they open possibilities of being and expression, it can also be an instrument for perpetuating inequalities, exploitation, abuse, and isolation. Playing software is not always "good" or desirable. Sometimes the things we play with turns us into "things"; they play us and deprive us of choice in the name of pretended freedoms and joys. That is why we need an ethos of digital play.

Playing Software was born on the realization that my experience with video games was quite strange. As a scholar in game studies, I spent long periods of time in virtual worlds, playing but also just hanging out. I realized I was feeling nostalgia for those worlds, not just for their geographies or the stories they contained, but also for the person I was in those games and how those games saw me. I missed being who I was in *Fallout 3* or *World of Warcraft*.[1] I also realized that as video games started being less present in my professional interests, I started playing them as a form of ritualized engagement with a particular mode of acting. For most of 2020, I played the game *Slay the Spire* once a day, in a ritual of learning to think as the Spire wants me to think and understanding how the system *acts*.[2]

Reflecting on my own practices of play made me realize that the kind of cultural and ethical understanding I derived from playing video games extended to all kinds of software and that relating to software through play has cultural consequences. Siri and Alexa are playful companions that also listen to us in moments of crisis, even if they are at heart surveillance devices with troublesome gender politics. Tesla cars have built in small, useless surprises—a sort of video game–inspired Easter egg—for users who perhaps want to see their car driving on Mars on the display console or turned into a mobile party. Artificial intelligence is less threatening when it is presented as an Animoji. And social media offer a stage where performance is rewarded with points in the shape of likes and shares. Where there is a computer, there is play.

To understand that argument, I will propose some variations on old media and concepts of play studies. For example, I will use *interface* to describe the meeting point between human and digital artificial agency. An interface will be the location where a new world comes into being. Similarly, I will propose the concept of *plaything* to describe the nature of the material and computational things involved in digital play.

These concepts become useful when I apply this way of looking to observe different manifestations of playing software. First, I will argue that make-believe is essential for understanding digital play. In fact I propose that it is pretense that drives playful engagements with software. Second, I will analyze the concept of systems, inquiring on the importance of cybernetic theory of digital play and how combining it with Lugones's ethos of play, we could study the ludic element in online conspiracy theories. Third and final, I will situate digital play in the context of contemporary capitalism, with a critique of the instrumentalization of play as a vehicle for platform capitalism.

This book is structured in two conceptual parts: chapters 1 through 3 focus on proposing the backbone of a theory of digital play. Chapters 4 through 6 apply that theory to different digital phenomena. I close the book in chapter 7 with a reflection on the challenges ahead from the perspective of digital play as an ethical engagement with software.

I have selected an ensemble cast to illustrate the relation among software, play, and culture. Treating software as actors is essential for the arguments I am going to make.[3] This is an argument that draws on science and technology studies, a field that has already argued for the importance of understanding the nonhuman agency of technology.[4] Software *acts*: for us, with us, at us, but also when we're not around.[5] It takes decisions in a world of its own; it writes the stories of that software world, it follows instructions, and yet it can also be open for improvisation and re-creation. As the philosopher of technology Mark Coeckelberg argues, computers can be understood as actors, because software follows lines and procedures, sometimes diverging from them, catastrophically or genially.[6] Like actors, software seems to be able to acquire a personality and present itself in one or multiple ways, forcing us to decipher their acting personas. And finally, like actors, software also *plays*—not just roles, but all other forms of specific ways of acting in the world.

One of the main actors in this book is voice assistant software like Alexa, Siri, and the Google Assistant. Voice assistants are interesting because the modality of interaction with them, the voice, does not necessarily provoke the same work-related evocations as keyboards and mice.[7] We have always *talked* to computers, not always by typing, but now they can understand us and talk back. Siri and Alexa pretend to have a personality, and we play along, treating them as *characters*.[8]

Another important actor is the software used for the quantified-self lifestyle. Step trackers, smart watches—any other device that senses our bodies, tracks our behaviors, and helps us live a more healthy lifestyle—all give us rules to live by and structure our lives one sensor at a time. The form of play here is also based on make-believe—on the (voluntary, though not always so) acceptance of these rules so that we can conform to the parameters that allow us to live in these worlds. Quantified self technologies show how rules upheld by software create worlds that we are inserted and how sometimes the design of these technologies uses play to ease our way into accepting that particular world.[9]

This book is also interested in forms of "playful design," from gamification to aesthetic-driven user experiences of conventional software.[10] During some of the years I was researching for this book, playful software seemed to be about to be the next thing, enhancing our experiences of software with pleasurable interactions. Physics-based graphical user interfaces with animations that highlighted every action were the staple of smartphone experience design, like Apple's "fluid interfaces." Screens usually dedicated to boring topics like banking became packed with movement and dynamism. Other potentially ludic experiences, like dating, became playfully creepy thanks to smooth interactions, swiping left and right until choices overwhelmed us.[11] This software, all of it actors, and is part of the cast of this book.

I am writing about play, and therefore it is also inevitable to write about video games because what are these games if not the privileged design form for digital play? As adults, when we think about playing with computers, we usually involve video games. These games are software made for playing, and therefore they are critical to understanding the play element in computational culture. There will also be video games in this book, but I will look at them as playable software, following the ideas behind Boluk and LeMieux's *Metagaming*.[12]

Finally, one of the most important actors is also the most shape-shifting of them all: the internet—that vast network of computers that serves us with memes and gifs, that makes us spend money and vent our opinions out loud to the world. From the expressiveness of the browser canvas to the Cthulhian dreads of submarine cables and data centers, the internet is a central actor in computational culture. Of course, the internet is not (just) software. But there is nothing more central to computational culture than the internet, not just as a technical system but also as a cultural-technical assemblage, a protean creature formed by the lives of cultures and human and software communities. The internet is the primordial soup of computational culture, the place where new agents and expressions emerge and evolve.

This book provides a ludic lens to study software. This means that the concepts and arguments presented here could also be applied beyond the scope of this cast of actors. When and where do we find play in software, then? Proper software uses the resources of machines as efficiently as possible so the results are achieved quickly, and without waste. Functionality and efficiency are the main values of proper software. And thus, any time we find *purposefully designed inefficiencies* or any time software is used in a *purposefully inefficient* way, we will find play. Eric Gordon has described play and playable media as being "meaningfully inefficient," an idea that powerfully translates Bernard Suits's philosophy to the information age.[13]

If we want to apply the ludic lens to software, the starting point is to identify and observe these meaningful inefficiencies. Play will manifest itself in our relations with software when the world we meet is less than efficient, when there are whimsical possibilities to shape and be shaped by computer programs. These inefficiencies can be designed for, like the personalities of AI voice assistants, or they can be the outcome of playful explorations of rigid systems. Playing software happens when form follows fun.

I want this book to be a provocation. I have written it with the goal of providing a direction of travel. I am taking some risks with my arguments. Claiming that digital play is unlike nondigital play might make me sound like a technological determinist. Trying to shift the central position of Huizinga in the canon of play theory implies breaking away from my own work and historied tradition in many disciplines. Arguing that make-believe is more important that competitive play in a world full of points and scores might seem foolish.

And yet we live in a world that is absolutely unlike the world in which classic theories of play were written. It's not just because there is software, but also because we have become aware of the effects of capitalism, colonialism, and the patriarchy in the very concept of "the canon." And this means that we have an opportunity to establish something new—building on the past because we cannot afford to be ahistorical creatures, but building on a past so we can have different futures.

Playing, analog and digital, is an instantiation of possibilities, a creation of possible worlds so we can live in them. This book wants to be a form of playing too. It wants to create a novel way of thinking about play for those of us who live in digital societies. This book wants readers—you—to be provoked; it wants readers to argue against it or with it, to break it and put it together. I want this book to be a voice in a constellation of work that knows that the only way we can make sense of and survive in a world of software is if we start playing.

1
Playing

It all starts with a blank screen.

In 2019 I released an iOS app called ATTN. It's a fairly simple thing: a white screen that slowly fades to black. If the user taps on the screen or swipes up, full brightness will be restored. ATTN is the first software I published on Apple's App Store, a walled garden where Apple users can find all kinds of what Apple touts as "quality software." A lot of that software promises to help users start living a better life through app-driven meditation, self-tracking, and learning. I'm sure, certain, and convinced that because ATTN was released in the App Store, I have contributed to saving the world, increased overall human well-being, and changed the direction of history.

I am also sure that the only thing ATTN does is play: it plays with the context of the App Store and its palettes of commodified well-being; it plays with software as an instrument to "solve" problems; it plays with software itself, making very complicated something that is deadly simple: dimming a screen. My goal with ATTN was to make something that was fun, a conceptual joke, the software equivalent of a pun. I wanted to laugh at what makes our society consider that software is so serious, so transcendental, so *important*. ATTN is playing software.

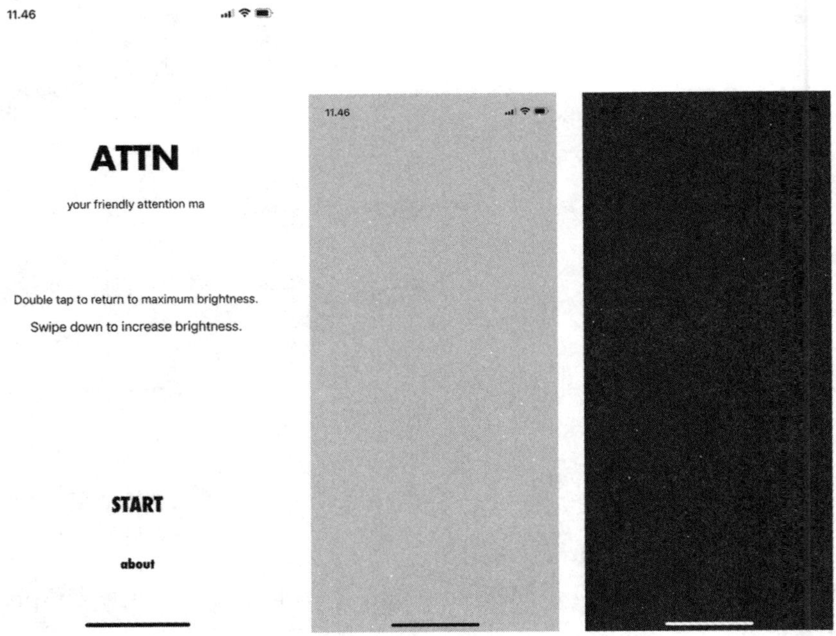

Figure 1.1
Three stages of ATTN. Author's screenshot.

To understand the cultures of the information age, we need to understand what happens when playing with software. We need to be able to make sense of why we play with computers, why play is so important when thinking, making, and engaging with software. Otherwise we may take it too seriously and think that everything can be solved with an app, even if it is just a blank screen. Why do we want software to be playful? Why do we want inhuman work to feel more bearable dressing it up as a game?

We play with software because software, like play, creates worlds. We play with software because playing is a way of relating to other forms of agency, and software creates forms of human and artificial agency. We play with software because it is fun—fun to use what is meant to be efficiently functional only in useless ways and fun to temporarily meet and become others in another world.

A premise for this argument is that digital play is significantly different from nondigital play. Stephanie Boluk and Patrick LeMieux argue that video games are not games, because "videogames conflate the rules of the game with the mechanics of the equipment."[1] I take this idea a bit further and claim that digital play is different from analog play because digital play is a relational mode of entangling with software agencies in the worlds created by and for software.

In this sense, digital play is a phenomenon of the information age. I am using the general concept of the information age following philosopher Luciano Floridi's terminology but also extending the insights that Lyotard presented in his analysis of knowledge in postmodernity.[2] When I mention the information age I refer to the historical time in which computers have become part of the fabric of (developed) societies. There are computer programs everywhere, letting us do things, forbidding others, suggesting what to do and what to buy, finding us partners, entertaining us, enriching us or making us poorer. And software is doing that not just to us: these programs are engaged in thriving exchanges of information imperceptible by our biological senses. Software relates to us but also to all other things, living and artificial. In the information age, a dying biosphere is entangled with a thriving infosphere, an environment in which human and software coexist.[3]

Many human-software relations in the infosphere are playful. There are video games, promising the pleasures of immersive synthetic worlds with their logics of empowerment and belonging. There are digital playgrounds, from *Minecraft* to Snapchat and Facebook and Instagram, that facilitate new places to live in with new mediated modes of relating to others.[4] There are also digital toys, from the venerable Tamagotchi or the always pleasing Alexa, to the more fluid, toy-like experiences of applications that want us to have fun while we bank, date, or post our lives online.[5] The infosphere can be a playful place, and playing software creates new forms of culture, art, and social relations.

Digital play is a mode of shaping subjectivities, drawing boundaries, and expressing and creating cultural forms as we relate to software agencies.[6] Play and software use rules and procedural logics to create worlds.[7] The rules of a game, when enacted, create the world of a game. The procedures of a particular piece of software create the world in which that software has agency.

I understand the concept of "world" as an environment in which certain modes of agency shape the experience of being. This multiplicity of worlds as settings for agency should not be new: the world of work is different from the social world, which is different from the family world. They may overlap, but they are different worlds in which we are different agents. These worlds are created through action, by doing things, but also by setting boundaries and procedures that delimit agency in meaningful ways. A work contract defines your agency at work. Loving someone shapes our agency too. We all live in many worlds, and some of those worlds are created for and by software. And in some of those software worlds, we play.

Presenting a world as a world in which we can play can change our agency in them. When Robinhood, an app designed to allow individuals to participate in the stock market, uses game design techniques like virtual confetti to celebrate the users' first investment, it is making a mundane activity feel more like play.[8] The confetti feature, as well as the dynamic visual experience of the app, draws heavily on the visual and game feel rhetorics of games.[9] Robinhood wants its users to experience trading as if it was a game, because then the agency of those participating in that experience is also defined as a playful agency. The nature of the stock market as presented in this app becomes close to that of a game, or a playground, and the agency of users becomes closer to that of what we would call "players."

Robinhood is designed to help anyone participate in the stock market. The way the software is designed facilitates that mode of agency by making it feel more like play. And when trading stocks becomes more playful, new cultural phenomena begin to take place. For example, at the time of writing this chapter, the video-sharing network TikTok hosted many popular investment videos that made use of Robinhood's playful rhetorics. In this new ecosystem of apps and media, trading stocks becomes shared in video platforms thanks to trading software designed to feel playful.

Writing about play implies invoking the work that Johan Huizinga started in 1938 with *Homo Ludens*. His central argument was deceptively simple: at the heart of culture is a play drive that shapes cultural manifestations and societies. There have been critical readings of this work,[10] as well as significant contributions that have extended "Huizingan play" to the information age, arguing that computationally mediated play is culturally significant and different from analog play.[11]

I will not be drawing on Huizinga for my understanding of playing software. The world has changed. We should understand play as not just a human, or other animal, phenomenon but as something that binds the human and the nonhuman together in productive ways. Huizinga's ideas were also driven by a conservative, European, imperialist drive. The culture he defined as being created by play was that of agonism—of well-regulated conflict among men, in particular, of a certain status and a certain origin. We don't live in that world anymore.

To play in the information age must not be to conquer others, human or not, through software. To play in the information age should be to acknowledge others, to thrive in the worlds we can create and travel along them and recognize others in them. We need an understanding of play in the information age that also has an ethos and a politics so we can better understand the ways play can be used as a form of control and manipulation.

Defining Play, Again (This Won't Be the Last Time)

The premise of this section on play is similar to that of *Homo Ludens*: play is the primordial source of culture from which phenomena like law, poetry, war, the arts, and language emerge. Playing software is then a primary source of the cultures of the information age.

Early theorists of software and culture already saw this happening: Turkle and Laurel understood the power of video games in the shaping of the nascent cultures around computers. I want to move beyond games to argue that playing is making sense of software in general.[12] Playing software is a *relational mode* of being in the world—a way of establishing, shaping, reshaping, and submitting to the relations that can be established between software agents and human agents.[13] In the course of playing software, new worlds are created in which artificial and human agency can relate. Some of these worlds will enslave us to the processes of computers; others will open up for the acting on what could be possible, for living in the possible and not in what is taken for granted.

In his brief reflection on play in *The Utopia of Rules*, David Graeber argues that there is more to play than following rules; in fact, "what ultimately lies behind the appeal of bureaucracy is fear of play."[14] But what play does bureaucracy fear? Graeber argues that a primordial, open-ended creative play that can create order *and* chaos is a better way to understand the pleasures of play and the importance of fun. We need a concept of play that accounts for different agencies and different worlds. At the same time, software can be used as a form of control, so we also need to think about the ethics of playing software. The theory of playfulness proposed by Argentinian philosopher María Lugones provides a solid foundation from which to understand playing in the information age.[15]

First, let's break with the past. Lugones provides a concise and scalding critique of Huizinga and, by extension, of most play theory. She argues that this tradition of play theory limits playfulness to something that has ultimately "to do with contest, with winning, losing, battling," an attitude she argues is incompatible with what she thinks is essential to play: the capacity to travel across "worlds."[16]

Lugones does not define *worlds* but provides a series of characteristics that can be used to identify them.[17] It is a world inhabited by people, imaginary or not; it may have a given society that has a culture and "a constructions of the relationships of production, of gender, race, etc."[18] A world "may be incomplete in that things in it may not be altogether constructed or something may be constructed negatively (they are not what 'they' are in some other 'world')."[19] Worlds construct agencies. My use of the concept of world is derived from this understanding of world: we, the human and the nonhuman, live in different worlds, and playing is relating to each other in those worlds. In doing so, we shape who we are or who we want to be.

For Lugones, the capacity to be different selves is "traveling" between worlds. Traveling is a shift to being another person, a shift that "may not be willful or even conscious."[20] Worlds construct the self that travels to them. Traveling matters because it allows us to think about which worlds we are at ease in, which worlds we like to inhabit. According to Lugones, playfulness constructs a self at ease in a world. Without playfulness, "I am not a healthy being in the 'worlds' that construct me unplayful."[21] Importantly, for Lugones, playfulness is "the attitude that I recommend as the loving attitude in travelling across 'worlds.'"[22]

In other words, playing is a mode of traveling between worlds in which we construct who we are so we can meet others. And in our meeting them, they also change who they are. Playfulness is defined by a loving attitude, which Lugones describes to a certain detail:

> So, positively, the playful attitude involves openness to surprise, openness to being a fool, openness to self-construction or reconstruction and to construction or reconstruction of the "worlds" we inhabit playfully. Negatively, playfulness is

> characterized by uncertainty, lack of self-importance, absence of rules or a not taking rules as sacred, a not worrying about competence and a lack of abandonment to a particular construction of oneself, others and one's relation to them.[23]

ATTN is a way of playing software because it creates a (ridiculous) world in which the very limited agency of software (dimming the brightness of the screen) has to be met with curiosity, with openness to rethink the trust we put in software, with an understanding of how unimportant software can be. Starting at a screen that dims itself is reaching out to a silly, playful, joyful software agent that does not want to be taken seriously. And in doing so, it also helps articulate a critique of the faith in software-based solutions.

Play and playfulness are loving ways of world traveling—silly, fun, foolish, essentially focused on acknowledging and relating to others while we also let others relate to ourselves. Play and playfulness are relational ways of lovingly traveling to others and becoming entangled with them. Play is movement, but not the to-and-fro of Gadamer's hermeneutics, which Lugones also considers to be an imperialist mode of play.[24] Lugones's movement is one of moving toward others, of loving perception of others. The essence of play should be to travel to others' worlds so "we can understand what is to be them and what it is to be ourselves in their eyes. Only when we have travelled to each other's 'worlds' we are fully subjects to each other."[25]

This idea of play has constructivist echoes that might evoke the work of Goffman and especially the understanding of play from a Goffmanian perspective that Stenros and Deterding have championed.[26] While their work and this book are interested in similar phenomena, I have taken Lugones as the foundational work because it allows me to draw on a philosophy of agency that relates well to involving the human and the nonhuman and that comes with an ethics for emancipatory play. Playing software is more than a social situation. It is world making and world traveling, reaching out to others and drawing others to us.

ATTN might be ridiculous, but in that ridiculousness, it exemplifies playing software.[27] Many apps promise us to solve our problems by tracking data we produce, by giving us a way of escape or to "connect" with others, and by doing so, they force us toward worlds where our interactions become limited. If we do what the software wants us to do, we will become fitter, happier, stronger. ATTN makes the absurdity of that claim evident by creating a ridiculous world that accepts only ridiculous forms of agency. Interacting with a blank screen is reaching an absurd world created by software that solves no problems and that by doing so will, I hope, make us laugh and realize the ridiculousness of all the promises of app stores and tech gurus. Playing ATTN is making sense of the futility of software, of the fact that all software is in itself ridiculous, even if some of it is useful.

This concept of play is close to posthumanist and cyborg theory,[28] and the type of relationality that Lugones writes about is close to the notion of entanglements of materialities and agencies that defines new materialist philosophy.[29] While new materialisms will be essential in chapter 3, when I describe what playing does to things and materials, it is worth stating now that the characteristics of such entanglements are fun and joy and pleasure, a relation of healthy skepticism toward rules and order and the possibility of becoming others in other worlds.

Let's look at this phenomenon through the perspective of video game, understood as software designed for playing. Blizzard might have produced *World of Warcraft*, but it is us, the players, who used that object and turned it into a world. It was a world of the players, facilitated by software. Video game worlds are worlds in which we are together—human and software deeply interrelated, shaping each other by playing. Borrowing Doug Wilson's terminology and invoking the work of Bernie DeKoven, there is a togetherness in the worlds created in play: togetherness with other agents, human or not.[30] There cannot be play without the togetherness of human and nonhuman agents.

C. Thi Nguyen has argued that games are the art form of agency.[31] I think Nguyen's position is essential not only to understand the aesthetics of games but also the nature of play. Playing is practicing agencies across worlds, and digital play is practicing agencies related to software agencies. I am departing here from Lugones's philosophy in that for her, playing is creating and meeting other subjectivities. While I agree that playing is creating subjectivities, as I argued in *The Ethics of Computer Games*, my intention here is to look at playing software. Software cannot claim to have a subjectivity or "inner life," but it can be argued that it has agency.[32] This is a rather instrumentalist approach that assumes that agency does not necessarily require internal mental states. My account of agency is performative and relational, that is, agency is the property of an agent that can act in relation to other agents and an environment.[33] Therefore, in my adaptation of Lugones's theory, world traveling is a process of developing and meeting forms of agency; more specifically, playing software is world traveling to meet the agency of software and establish reciprocal relations with it. In the next section, I explain in more detail the agency of software.

Playing as world traveling is closely related to the exploration of boundaries. Nippert-Eng argues that boundary play is "a sequential, layering activity focused on the potential, alternative (re)drawings of the boundary at hand" and that it most often takes place in the context of "classificatory boundaries."[34]. Digital play is boundary play because it is a constant engagement with forms of human and artificial agency, their boundaries, and the very nature of the worlds in which these relations take place.

For example, the complex relations between players and their digital avatars in video games illustrate how part of the appeal and the fun of digital play is the exploration of the actual boundaries of the self when entangled with software systems.[35] It could also be argued that the "quantified self" movement is also a form of digital play that explores the pleasures and pains of understanding the boundaries of bodies as perceivable by software, as *computable*. This exploration of boundaries can be joyful, if the ethos of Lugones's playfulness succeeds and there is a skepticism of rules. But it can also be tyrannical if the boundaries are imposed under the promises of fun but the purpose is, for example, to make underpaid labor more palatable.

In play, the relations with other agents are negotiated, not imposed. We can always decide to stop playing. We are not necessarily driven by productivity, results, outcomes, or the conditions of other worlds we live in. Playing can be a form of emancipation from all those other worlds in which the goals, the purpose, and the meaning are externally imposed, like work.

Playing is world traveling, for pleasure, with curiosity, not taking things for granted and ready to laugh and have fun. The purpose of the activity of play can be defined externally, by the boundaries created in the act of relational appropriation, and internally, by the expressive relations facilitated by those boundaries. These are the boundaries of new worlds. The concept of play that informs my understanding of digital play is driven by these ideas of world traveling, of togetherness in the exploration of boundaries, and of fun as enacting desirable possibilities. Whether it is playing a video game or toying around with software, digital play is a meeting point to negotiate the joys and pleasures between human and software agencies.

Embracing Lugones's ethos of loving world traveling is central to my project because there are forms of digital play that are not loving or constructive. They are fun, but there is also fun in cruelty and in the imposition of boundaries on others. To be precise: the embodied pleasures of playful pain are play as long as they are consensual, agreed on, and a way of world traveling.[36] But there are forms of engaging with software and its worlds that look like play that also promise fun, but are in fact manipulations of agency for submission.

For example, play can be a way of becoming conservative and embracing the ethos and economics of platforms. The embrace of competitive quantification of emotional engagement that Facebook and Twitter, through their "like" and "heart" functions, facilitate makes us subject to their platforms.[37] This form of trivializing opinion and emotional response dilutes engagement and reflection and turns reading and writing about life and the world into a competition to get the right number of predetermined, rule-based responses. An alternative that illustrates this form of nefarious digital play is a playful approach to this rule set, proposed by the artist Ben Grosser with his Facebook Demetricator, a tool that eliminates the visual representation of reactions in these platforms (figure 1.2). The demetricator empowers users to draw their boundaries, to negotiate their relation to the agency of software based not on the agonistics of quantification but on other parameters. The demetricator facilitates world traveling, even with technological platforms that live off pleasurably restricting forms of agency.

Lugones gives the concept of digital play an ethos. Digital play requires the loving attitude in world traveling, the acknowledgment of the other as a foundation for playing. Other forms of world traveling can be fun, but there's fun in cruelty and in oppression for those who are oppressors. Digital play ought to be founded on this loving relation between biological and artificial agencies. Later in the book, I critique forms of digital play that do not respect

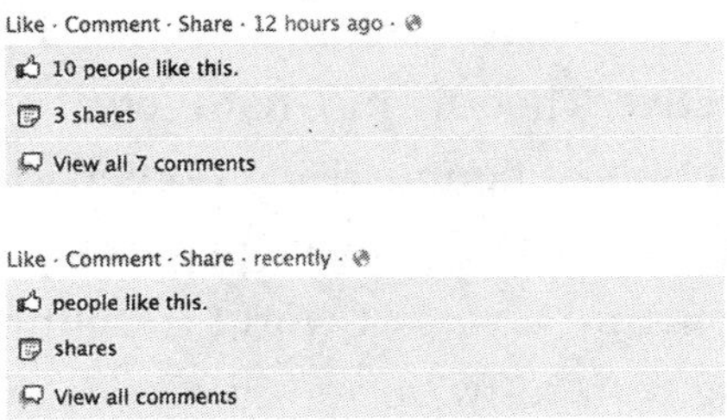

Figure 1.2
The Facebook Demetricator. Screenshot by Ben Grosser.

this ethos, and by doing so I sketch an ethics and politics of digital play.

Play articulates new worlds, opens up for new relations, makes us travel between worlds. Donna Haraway stated that "through playful engagement with each other, we get a hint of what can still be and learn how to make it stronger."[38] Playing software can be a form of emancipatory alliances facilitated by software agencies. But it can be so only if it lives up to the ethos of world traveling, particularly to not taking rules as sacred because digital play is a phenomenon of an age of control and rules, of an age of software.

Software Agents

In most of the world, the increased presence of computers has changed the way we create knowledge, relate to others, elect people, or create artistic works. If we want to think society, or culture, or even humanity, we need to consider how they relate to machines. Following Haraway, our present is that of the cyborg, identities in flux entangled with other agents, human and not, that shape us and are shaped by us. Software creates this world and contributes to shape its agencies.

What is software? I use *software* as a generic term that encompasses programs with instructions that allow computers to process data and perform operations. Since this is not a book about what computation is, I have gone for a definition that is clear, simple, and moderately simplistic. My understanding of computation is informed by Philip Agre's work and Warren Sack's recent application of Agre's in *The Software Arts*.[39] In the narrow sense I am using in this book, software is any program running on a computing machine. These programs are constituted by data that represent *something* and instructions and rules to perform operations on those data.

The concept of computational agency is drawn from Floridi's *The Philosophy of Information*. Essentially, on a given level of abstraction, a computational system can be said to have agency. Establishing that level of abstraction is what we do when we play: we select parts of the world as relevant for playing and ignore the rest. Software agency takes place as a world in which human and software actions relate and have an effect on each other. When software performs actions that have an effect on humans, we have software agency. Because we live in the information age, more and more of our human experience implies relating to software agency, from politics to social relations. Sometimes the physical world changes to allow for artificial agency, when, for example, surfaces display QR codes readable only by machines or when cities slowly adapt to self-driving vehicles and the way they see the world.

Agency starts with data, because computer programs perform operations on data. Inspired by Floridi's *The Philosophy of Information* and Goriunova's article about "people as data as persons," I understand data as the outcome of a process of representation.[40] A computer, for example, has representations of different numbers, from integers to floating point numbers, and also of characters that might form strings if put together. We can make data structures that represent more complicated things, like arrays and lists, or custom data types structures that better formalize what is being represented. Computers are machines that perform operations on these data. This capacity to perform operations on data that represents something is what makes software an agent. Data represent the world so that computers can act. When we create representations with data processed in a program by a computer, we are instantiating a world where software has agency.

Let's look at step trackers as examples. A step tracker uses software that reads data from different sensors and outputs a qualitative evaluation of a user's motion: how many steps taken during the day, how many miles run, and more. Step trackers are interesting because they have an effect on bodily practices—the way imperfect data are read from imperfect sensors is translated in an evaluation of embodied activity. That embodied activity is then modified to fit the requirements of the step tracker: we walk, or run, so that the sensor can track the data. Of course, sensors and software are becoming better at reading motion, but as expert athletes know, changing body motion to achieve optimal results often involves acting in the way a machine suggests acting. But we don't need the example of professional athletes: Why do we walk ten thousand steps? Why do we follow the advice of "health" apps? Why do we sleep the way sleep trackers want us to? We do so partially because this software, acting in the world, changes what sleeping, walking, and running are. These activities become computable processes, and we become data producers relating to data processing software.

A computational world, an infosphere, entangles human and software agency. This entanglement also requires forms of "enveloping" the world so that computers can act in it.[41] For example, we change typographies or layouts so they become machine readable, or we use textured surfaces so augmented reality applications can better display their worlds in them. We can imagine examples of oppressive algorithms that create a world that only some can inhabit: worlds of white patriarchies built on racist software agents.[42] In that world, some humans will be lesser agents because of the agency of software. Once again, entangling with software requires an ethos and a politics; otherwise, the faith in computational agency as objective, rational, and "scientific" will produce monsters.

I like to think (and the sooner the better!) of software as an alien agency materialized in computers, diffused in networks, and distributed in the infrastructure of the everyday. Instead of thinking about software as an instrument or tool, and instead of framing it using the parameters we use to try to explain artificial intelligence, we should think of software as being a form of agency absolutely different to ours. This is what I mean by alien agency: software acts in the world in ways we cannot make sense of exclusively by thinking of it using the parameters of human agency. Joseph Weizenbaum wrote: "However much intelligence computers may attain, now or in the future, theirs must always be an intelligence alien to genuine human problems and concerns."[43]Software operates with its own logic, often within black boxes that hide its intentions, possibilities, and capabilities[44]. Relating to these alien agencies is one of the main challenges of the information age.

Here's where the role of play becomes clear. Alexa, Siri, and the Google Assistant are programmed to react to nonfunctional statements like "sing me a song" or "tell me a joke," so they can ease the acceptance of their alien agency as part of our domestic, mundane landscapes. It's a pretense that these alien agencies can relate to "genuine human problems and concerns." If the voice assistant responds to jokes, if it seems to have a sense of humor, if we can play with it, we can make sense of it. We can make mistakes and it won't punish us, because it's no longer a machine with a function that we may operate incorrectly. Voice assistants are playthings that reward our curiosity and let us imagine that what we're interacting with is not the end point of a deep well of technology and infrastructure and money but *someone* we can relate to. We pretend, we engage in make-believe, we play (together) with software.

When software operates and acts on data representations of the world, we can talk about software agency. This agency is perceived as alien, and therefore it needs modes of relating to it. In our terminology, it needs possibilities to travel to its worlds. Because software operates with rules and processes and play is also a matter of rules and processes, play becomes a mode of making sense of software agency. We play with software to make sense of its alien agency.

Playing Software

In *Computer Power and Human Reason,* Weizenbaum describes how the information age is not only a consequence of the ubiquitous presence of computers in the world, but also that it is a transition time in history from which it is not possible to return: "The computer becomes an indispensable component of any structure once it is so thoroughly integrated with the structed, so enmeshed in various vital substructures, that it can no longer be factored out without fatally impairing the whole structure."[45] Weizenbaum also identifies how software creates worlds in which software has agency and how the programmer, like the game designer, is a maker of worlds: "The computer programmer, however, is a creator of universes for which he alone is the lawgiver. So, of course, is the designer of any game. But universes of virtually unlimited complexity can be created in the form of computer programs. Moreover, and this is a crucial point, systems so formulated and elaborated *act out* their programmed scripts. They compliantly obey their laws and vividly exhibit their obedient behavior."[46]

Weizenbaum understood how software creates worlds and how these worlds are the consequence of programming software agencies. He argued that these worlds are "detached from the real world in the same way that every abstract game is."[47] The ethical challenge of software is how the worlds it creates relate to the needs, values, wishes, and demands of people—and also of other species and of the planet. Computers create worlds that are conceived and run within programs in machines. These worlds have also become our worlds. The ethical, cultural, and technical challenge of the software age is to relate to software agencies and their worlds.

I started this chapter mentioning ATTN, my humorous app that consists of a white screen that progressively blacks out. ATTN was designed to "substitute" the incessant stream of content we consume on mobile devices. Social media is nothing but a deluge of news and updates that requires little more than a gesture to flood us more and more content. That is the agency of that software: the constant connection to others at our command. ATTN makes fun of that by eliminating content in an effort to make obvious that what matters in social media is not the stories we see, the people we connect to, but the entanglement with software that wants us to consume more, to stay updated, to keep the screen on to keep our attention properly monetized. ATTN allows a form of world traveling to a ridiculous take on the software agencies that captivate our attention. It is an application of Lugones's ideas, an app designed with a playful, joyful, and humorous take on the processes of software and the way we accept its rules to create new worlds.

Designers and developers understand that play is used to relate to the agency of software. Play becomes an instrument to provide specific forms of engagement. For example, social media applications are designed to make the refresh mechanisms easy to learn and rewarding, like the infamous "pull to refresh" action. Play adds pleasure to the processes of relating to software. This can also lead to negative applications of play. For example, behavioral tracking can be creepy until we turn it into a competition.[48] Tracking our steps and movements is surveillance until it becomes a competitive game of self-improvement, like those offered by services like Endomondo or Strava. Vast networks of surveillance capitalism are creepy until we give them a name and a personality and Alexa soothes us into new needs.[49] Software can be creepy, until we play with it.

I want to stress the importance of embracing Lugones's ethos. I want to think about play in the information age as a loving attitude toward the computational world. We have had enough of play and order and rules and victories. World traveling as a loving attitude is a relational engagement with the world that allows us to experience joy and fun, engaging with software for the sheer pleasure of engaging with it. Play should not be the exclusive domain of people like me: straight, white European men who have been raised in the rhetorics of dominance and victory at play. I want to ally with Lugones's work because she shows the importance of fun as a way of meeting other agencies and creating other possible worlds as a place where we meet others and have fun together.

In the information age and in the Anthropocene, we need a theory of play that reflects the multiple practices of play, from games[50] to the playful relations between species.[51] Play as loving world traveling lets us inquire, enjoy, and question the software-driven worlds in ways that open up for everybody, biological or artificial, to play.

The challenge of understanding digital play and its ethics is to specify what we mean by loving. Throughout this book, examples of healthy world traveling illustrate how play can be a form of exploring, expanding, and relating to others through modifications of our agency. Digital play can be a liberating and emancipatory form of practicing new forms of agency in a world of software. Playing software can be daring to create new worlds that embrace multiple forms of agency, worlds that are real because we play in them.

Throughout this book, I deal with examples in which digital play becomes an instrument of conquest and agonistic submission. Lugones's world traveling presupposes a loving attitude to others. But sometimes world traveling seduces with the pleasures, the fun of becoming submitted or to make others submit to rules. In his easy "What's the Point If We Can't Have Fun?" David Graeber warns about the possibility of cruel and destructive activities being fun.[52] Play should be fun, liberating, surprising, enjoyable, because it means loving world traveling and creating a new world with others. If that fun is at the expense of others, if that fun requires subjecting others to our whims, or not recognizing others, it is fun, but it is not play. And this might be a challenge for play scholars: What do we do with the forms of play that are fun for some because they are hurtful for others? Later in this book, I suggest that the concept of *plaything* can be used to make sense of what happens to people as they become objectivized when playing.[53]

Maybe others will consider that form of conquering, Huizingan play, a form of pleasure. The legacy of Huizingan play is strong in our understanding of play. Even the most interesting contemporary theories of play, from C. Thi Nguyen's reflections on agency and striving play[54] to the Goffmanian accounts of play and playfulness,[55] are hesitant in their thinking of play as a phenomenon beyond games. I want to think of playing as something else: as a form of relating to other forms of agency, human and nonhuman, biological and computational. Playing is a way of acknowledging the existence of other agents, and loving play is a way of finding the pleasure in the productive, fun, curious experience of other agents. To me, this means that even competitive play cannot be reduced to winning or succeeding. Playing is not an excuse to reproduce rhetorics of domination. Playing is meeting others, human or not, relating to them, and creating something new together.

With this ethos, let's start untangling what happens when we play software. If playing software is entangling with artificial agencies and the world they create, the next step is to understand what happens at that point of encounter. The worlds of play and software meet at the interface, and that is where we are headed now.

2

Interfaces

In this chapter, I think through the argument that the world created by the play-driven entanglement of biological and computational agency is a location in which we can observe the effects of playing in the information age. In other words, it is time to write about magic circles. Otherwise, how would a book about play be respectable?

The magic circle idea has a long and fraught history in play and game studies.[1] This concept describes how play takes place separate from the rest of the world—in a different physical place, like a stadium, but also in a different experiential frame in which the concerns of the mundane do not apply. This idea of play being separate from the real world can be extremely productive. In almost all definitions of play, the fact that playing takes place in an encapsulated time and space location seems to be essential to understand the phenomenon itself. Huizinga used the concept of magic circle to describe actual spaces, like stadiums and arenas. As play studies progressed, the concept of magic circle was extended to encompass the messy fact that play is both separated from the real world and connected to it. The concept became less useful as scholars began to observe the complex interrelations among the realities in play outside play. Goffman's concept of frames helped add nuance to the magic circle, particularly when thinking of the social aspects of playing.[2] The concept of magic circle is useful because it identifies that play happens in particular locations—both physical and virtual. Playing has its places, and it creates spaces. I propose that the spaces in which playing software takes place are the interfaces.

Playing software is world traveling so that human and software agencies can entangle, relate to, and make sense of each other. That relational engagement creates a world. The location of that world of playing is the interface. To explain the interface as meeting point, this chapter draws on postphenomenological theory, a philosophical approach to the mediating role of technologies in our experience of the world.[3] Following this tradition, I propose that the interface is the location in which the relational playing of human and software agents meets. That interface is what becomes observable when we study play and what is designed when we create playable software.

Thinking the Interface

The literature on the study of interfaces is extensive, particularly in media theory and human–computer interaction. However, my use of the concept of interface is a synthesis of the works of Vilém Flusser, Frederich Kittler, and especially Alexander Galloway's *The Interface Effect*.[4] That is, I am taking a media-studies-infused, postphenomenologically grounded understanding of what interfaces are, including the applications of these theories to video games.

In his reading of Flusser, Alexander Galloway argues that "interfaces are both surfaces and thresholds. On the one hand, an interface is a kind of surface screen, whether literal or figurative, that contains meanings and operations. On the other hand, an interface is a window or doorway that facilitates passage."[5] In *The Interface Effect*, Galloway takes this idea further, arguing that "the computer is not an object, or a creator of objects, it is a process or active threshold mediating between two states."[6] This idea informs my argument that the interface is the location of the entanglement between human and computational agencies.

Drawing on the work of Lucy Suchman and Julie Cohen, I consider that the act of being in the interface is a practice.[7] Drawing on Cohen's interpretation of De Certeau,[8] I consider being in the interface from the perspective of a tactics of adaptation to living entangled with artificial agencies, a form of everyday practice of the information age.[9] My understanding of playing as a practice in the context of video games is parallel to Brendan Keogh's and Stephanie Boluk and Patrick LeMieux's close readings of material practices in the context of video games.[10] Media scholars and sociologists have also looked at the role of materiality and agency in play.[11] My contribution here is to synthetize their works and situate these observations under a broader concept of interface as practice.

My understanding of the interface as a playing practice is closely related to Boluk and LeMieux's concept of metagaming, which describes specific ludic practices with video games, like video game modding, the act of creating variations of or new content for already existing digital games. Their work explores the critical and aesthetic possibilities emerging in the entanglement of human and artificial agency. For example, speed running is practicing the limits of what players can do to beat a video game. It is a way of modulating the agency of the player, adapting it to the requirements of a software agent so a set of goals can be achieved in the minimum possible time. Speed running does not necessarily understand software agency as something static, as fixed rules. Using glitches, shortcuts, and occasionally the very material aspects of computation, such as memory allocation, speed runners create playable worlds in which their relation with the agency of software is fluid and mutant. The place where those relations take place is the interface, a location in which speed running is possible.

But this book goes beyond video games. All forms of meeting between human and software agencies are practices. For example, drawing on the work of Gina Neff and Dawn Naffus, as well as on the radical critique of these interfaces proposed by Katta Spiel and Kathrin Gerling, I propose that self-tracking software is an interface that often uses play as an instrument that modulates human agency so it becomes acceptable by a software agent.[12] Motion or sleep trackers asks us to behave in such a way that sensors can detect and track our behavior, and they often do so through playful visualizations and competitive challenges. Self-tracking apps might be the opposite of speed running. If in speed running the human player bends artificial agents to make it easier to go faster in the world of a game, self-tracking applications are interfaces in which a software agent constrains human agency so it becomes faster, stronger, harder. The interface is the location in which biological and artificial agency meet. This interface is also a practice of entangling biological and artificial agencies.

First Steps

I was a runner for many years. Every morning I geared up to go out and run, always with the company of an audiobook and my iPod's or iPhone's step counter. Typically my goal would be to run 5 kilometers, choosing routes that looped close to home, and always stopping when the step counter told me that the distance was done. But here's the thing: I never ran 5 kilometers—I ran what my phone considered to be 5 kilometers, at the pace it could measure.

Of course, these devices are accurate, and they use a multiplicity of data sources to make sure that their 5 kilometers are actually 5 kilometers and that the pace they are showing is the actual pace of the run. But sensors are noisy, the world is a mess, and things get complicated when we add bodies to the computational mix. What matters here is that my practice of running was aided by software, and that aid led to a change of my behavior: instead of trusting road signs to measure my pace, I trusted the device. I ran what it told me was 5 kilometers. Most of the time, it worked wonders. But sometimes there were big differences in the measured times or distances. I always ran what the computer told me to run. I did not question it. My world became what the computer was measuring. My running practice was the practice of a series of algorithms.

Playing software is a process of meeting a software agent in a world where relations between the human and the computational are possible. In doing so, a new world is created where both agents can coexist. That world happens somewhere, and that somewhere is an interface, the point of encounter between computational agency and human agency. In the case of my motion tracker, the computer acts, measuring my activity and giving it particular meaning. When I relate to that agency, adjusting my own actions, I modify my agency so it becomes visible and relatable to the software agent. My human, physical step becomes whatever can be computed by an array of sensors and some algorithms. In the interface, I meet and relate to the agency of that software. I often did so by playing, making sense of that practice using the vocabulary and practices I learned from playing video games: acquiring points, unlocking achievements, competing for a high score.

When writing about the interrelation between playing, understood as world traveling, and software, understood as a ubiquitous form of artificial agency, we need to observe what happens at the point in which those two forms of agency meet. The concept of interface serves this purpose: it allows us to look into and dissect the point of contact between agents. In that meeting point, in the position of the interface, new practices emerge—playful practices of software. Playing software is the practice of engaging with software agencies in the meeting point of the interface. From that practice, social, cultural, and technical phenomena emerge.

The Practice of Playing Software

The concept of the play interface helps describe the relations established between software and human agency. Let's look at how computers see the world and what it means to engage with software that sees us.[13]

The capacity of computers to identify objects in visual data is relatively old, but it became a more visible part of culture when social media started offering their users the possibility to tag people on pictures, identifying their faces. In early 2019, Facebook's interface glitched and showed what the computer "sees" in the images on the site. The social, political, and ethical questions around object recognition and algorithmic bias are evident: who determines what a computer can "see" and how they do it.[14]

On the day of that breakdown, Facebook users were treated to a rare glimpse of the workings of the machinery of the site.[15] On some pictures, instead of loading the image file, the users saw an error displayed, together with a short description of what the image may contain, as seen by the machine vision systems of Facebook. In the screenshot in figure 2.1, the computer sees two people, probably sitting outdoors, probably smiling. Those are the data that the image posted by my friend feeds to the Facebook machine.

Machine vision is captivating, almost magical. Instant messaging applications offer filters that identify facial elements and substitute them with computer-generated graphics. Cars can drive autonomously because they can perceive the world, with senses beyond the human, even if they sometimes confuse people for things and things with people. Object recognition, powered by machine learning systems and vast image data sets, is an example of what software can do in the world. But what happens if we break object recognition software?

Drawing on Eric Gordon's idea of play and games being meaningfully inefficient, playing software can be understood as a productively

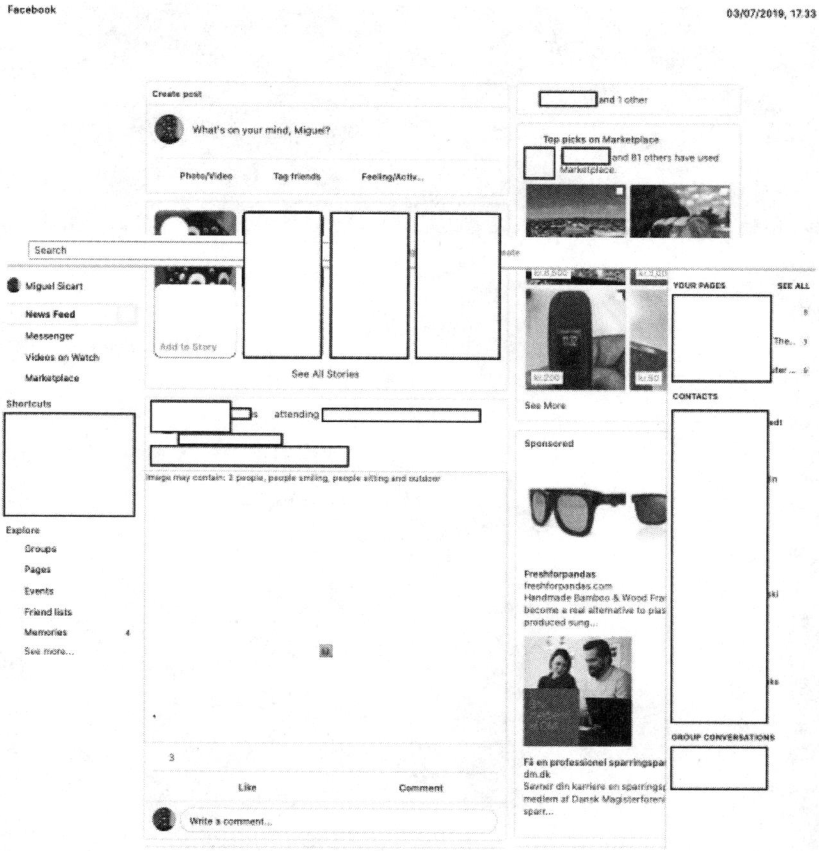

Figure 2.1
The Facebook interface behind the interface. Author's screenshot.

inefficient engagement with software.[16] Inefficiency was an aesthetic goal of my ridiculous software project Probably Not. Released in the last days of 2019, this app is a joke about artificial intelligence and its interest on making software that recognizes objects in the world.

Probably Not was designed with the specific intent of exploring how ridiculous and vain this submission to object recognition can be. It is a fairly simple program: it lets users take or select a picture with their phones, and then the software tells them what the main object in the picture probably is not (figure 2.2). Instead of

Figure 2.2
Probably Not at work. Author's screenshot.

recognizing objects for what they are, Probably Not tells users what the object in the picture they are seeing is not, with rather precise accuracy.

Built using Apple's toolchain and the Swift programming language, this ridiculous software filters the image that the user has selected through a machine learning function that returns an array of results, ranked in descending order based on the confidence of the prediction (figure 2.3). Typically, object recognition programs display the first result in that array. Probably Not returns the second or third result. These second guesses are useless and moderately funny. Probably Not is an object recognizer that tells the user what the main object in a picture is not, statistically speaking.

This embracing of inefficiency is the key for its playfulness. Probably Not explores the problems and relative silliness of delegating human perception to computers. It does not deny the importance of object recognition in some contexts, but it pokes fun at the inner workings of machine learning and its enchanted determinism, "a discourse that presents deep learning techniques as magical, outside the scope of present scientific knowledge, yet also deterministic, in that deep learning systems can nonetheless detect patterns that give unprecedented access to people's identities, emotions, and social character."[17] It is a form of play with computational media, one that makes fun of the agency of computers and the occasional faith we bestow on it when we meet it.

The humor in Probably Not, with apologies for explaining a joke, resides in how it uses inefficiency and error to let us reflect on the processes and possibilities of machine vision. Most software tells us what things are, how they should be, what to do, how to act. It imposes uses and practices because that is how things should be. Probably Not is built around the opposite idea: software is not good at telling us what things are but at calculating what things are likely not.

With Probably Not I tried to explore an extreme version of something that many of us, computer users, can recognize: playing around

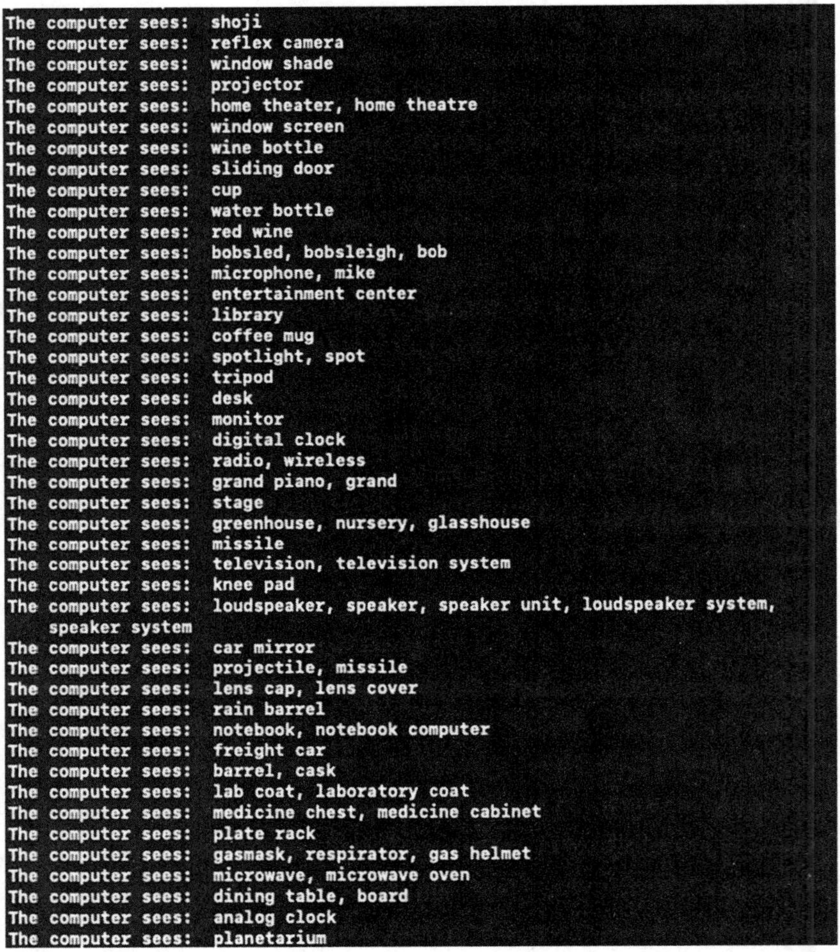

Figure 2.3
What the computer sees in Probably Not. Author's screenshot.

with software to see what we and it can do. Many of us tinker with menus and properties in a word processor or in an image processing program to figure out what kind of expression we can draw from these tools, what we can do with them. We toy around with photography apps so we can exploit the wonders of software-driven photography, creating impossible angles or lighting effects. We even program spreadsheet software to see what it can do, like playing games or proof that the Excel formula language is Turing complete (basically, we can use Excel to program anything without using another programming language).

We play with software because it can do things, and we need to explore that agency so we can relate to it. That exploration happens at the interface. This interface has always been present in our relation to software. We have even devised a particular type of software, video games, to explore the possibilities of that interface. Therefore, video games are a good place to understand how the concept of the play interface can be applied to the study of human practices with software.

Video Games as (Interface) Practices

Video games are software designed to create playable experiences. Software uses rules and processes to allow computers to perform operations on data representations, and video games use rules and processes to allow users to interact with computational models designed to create play. Video game design is the art of designing rules and processes that create arbitrary challenges that require skill, luck, or a combination of both, structuring the experience of the world created by that software. In this sense, video games are world engines. They create worlds in which computational agency is observable in the form of enemies, interactive challenges, and the visual representation of data that simulate environments. In these worlds, human agency is the outcome of rules that restrict action and mechanics that afford behaviors.[18]

Game studies popularized the study of games from a multidisciplinary perspective. Humanists, social scientists, and computer scientists have long argued about the cultural, emotional, ethical, and technical impact of video games. This book aligns with a tradition in game studies that looks at games in the broader context of the social and cultural changes consequence of the mass adoption of computers. Sherry Turkle, David Sudnow, Brenda Laurel, N. Katherine Hayles, Janet Murray, and Celia Pearce have written about the role of play in the software society, looking at games but also at other forms of play.[19] Instead of looking at games as objects, software, or designed elements, this tradition parallel and partially in game studies looked at games *as played*, or, more important for the argument in this book, it looked at games as *practices*. This argument is also indebted to Lucy Suchman's studies of the fluid relations established between humans and computational systems.[20]

Any time we interact with a video game, we are developing a practice. The way we sit in front of the PC or the console, the time of the day we prefer for playing, the controllers we like—they are all part of the material considerations of that practice.[21] Playing video games is also developing the practice of understanding the rules, figuring out how the game acts, how we can act in the game. It is making sense of what the software wants us to do and what we want to and can do. The pleasure of playing video games resides in developing these practices, and these practices shed light on how we develop relational practices with all kinds of software.

As an illustration, I'll share my own practices playing two different video games. I will describe my own practices of play, hoping that they will resonate with other players' experiences and practices. My practices are unique to me, yet at the same time, they contain others' practices. Readers who have played a video game can probably find their own emotions and reflections reflected in my observations, as I find myself doing when I read accounts of other people's playing. I have chosen mainstream video games with the hope of making my reflections relatable for as many players as possible, but I argue that all players can recognize the pleasures of playing a video game from a detailed account of another player, even if they are unfamiliar with the game itself. In any case, my focus here will be on my playing of *Into the Breach* and *FIFA*.[22]

I am not particularly fond of strategy games like *Civilization.*[23] They are professionally interesting, but I don't play them as part of my leisure. My taste often draws me to games that use procedurally generated content to create gameplay. By "procedurally generated content," I am referring to games that use semi-random or statistical processes to create, modify, or adapt the content of a video game from maps or avatars to their core gameplay.[24] The classic games with procedural generation are *Elite* and *Rogue*, and the most important game of the 2000s, *Spelunky.*[25]

I like procedurally generated content in games because it feels like the most thrilling point of contact with the agencies of software. The game changes, it adapts, it shows itself as a thing that has an intelligence of its own, looking at and evaluating the player. Playing games with procedural content generation is like meeting an octopus—witnessing the unfolding of an alien intelligence that observantly relates to you. Games designed around procedurally generated content are the most insightful playable media of the software age, for they reveal the agencies of computation while we playfully grapple with them.

That is why I enjoyed so much the video game *Into the Breach*, despite the fact that it was a real-time strategy game. This game uses procedural content generation sparingly to shift the maps and the spawn locations of the enemies. There is a story to the game, of course, but what matters about *Into the Breach* is the way in which it gives players a well-defined set of tools that require learning and rewards them with mastery in order to overcome procedurally generated challenges. In other words, *Into the Breach* gives players tools to master so they can explore their agency in the context of ever-changing playable environments.

In that intersection, my practice of play became meaningful. I played *Into the Breach* systematically, every available hour, for months. I enjoyed the gradual learning of the tools I was given, the different powers that the different vehicles in the game have, how they can be combined to create unexpected behaviors that will help me beat the scenario. I was getting better at playing the game. My practice of play was deeply related to the pleasure of getting better at playing this video game.

At the same time, that skill development was matched with procedurally generated environments. Levels were similar but never the same, and new enemies in these vaguely familiar environments required me to strategize how I could use different powers. Playing *Into the Breach* is observing how the agency of software manifests itself as a game. Part of my getting better at playing the game consisted of understanding how to observe, analyze, and adapt to this agency. I learned to see how the game would behave from the perspective of the skills I developed, but also from the perspective of the agency that the game allowed me to have. Submitting to the agency of the game gave me the satisfaction of realizing how to deal with the challenges proposed by that software with the tools that software gave me. Playing was fun because it forced me to shape my agency to the shifting shapes of procedural agency.

Video game design is the design of playable software that uses game-like structures to create a human experience. More specifically, video game design is the design of the interface, the meeting point between human and software agent. Video game designers use their skills to create a software agent that shapes and reacts to human agency. To design video games is to design forms of human and artificial agency and to design the place where they meet, the interface between both.[26]

We often talk about games from the perspectives of engagement and focus, praising how video games can captivate our attention and immerse us in other worlds. These games are engaging because they give us an access to the agency of software. As Nguyen argues, video games shape and contain human agency as specified by software.[27] They do so in a form that is pleasurable. Playing video games illustrates the role of play in the information age because it is the practice of developing skills generated by a system of rules and processes in order to shape human agency in the form that responds to the requirements of software. Playing video games is surrendering our agency to the worlds created by the games through rules and processes materialized in computational objects. In that surrendering, we learn to *see the alien,* to accept and adapt to the constraints and possibilities of the alien agencies of software. That's why so much software looks and feels to some extent a video game, from operating systems to mediation apps, because video games have taught us how and where to meet with the agency of software and how to have fun doing so.

Playing the soccer simulation *FIFA* illustrates the pleasurable practice of understanding artificial intelligence algorithms. I have been an avid player of this game since *FIFA 10* and have probably logged more hours with this game than with any other game. I have broken more controllers playing *FIFA* than what I will publicly admit (eleven). It is the game I play yearly, a companion, a practice of play that will follow me for years to come.

While doing research for this book, I got to thinking about what makes *FIFA* interesting to me. There is of course the interest I have in soccer, the most beautiful game. There is also the acknowledgment that I am (or used to be) pretty good at playing the game, which feels good. The bite-sized playing sessions are also important, in that the game adapts to my life. There is as well the pleasure of playing against real people, over the internet, matching skills and knowledge of the game, beating and being beaten to it.

But I realized that there is a particular thing I love about playing *FIFA* that makes me always return to it as an example of a prototypical game. From *FIFA 12* onward, the game has a defensive system that allows the player to control one avatar, while directing the artificial intelligence to mark the opposing team's players. In soccer terms, it allows the creation of two-on-one situations in defense, in which the human player can cover the passing lanes while the AI will press the opposing player who carries the ball. Essentially *FIFA* allows players to establish a joint action with the game's AI, with the goal of defending more efficiently.

Being good at *FIFA* is, among other things, being good at reading the tells from the AI: how your rival is delegating control to the AI, when a delegation is happening, when which animations will trigger, and so on. When I am matched with a player at my level or slightly above, many matches are won or lost based on one quick, adequate read of what decisions the AI is taking: Is my opponent covering the passing lanes or trying to overwhelm my player with defensive pressure? Is my opponent letting me progress in order to defend in a low block, letting the AI do the pressing while they cover the spaces? Or are they trying to press high up and retrieve the ball as soon as they lose it? If the defender controller by the AI rushes out, there will be space for a through pass—I make a run, a pass, and a goal because I have read the AI. At the same time, I have managed to win some matches against opponents better than I am because of the shared efforts of the game AI and mine, closing down passing possibilities thanks to a close collaboration between my AI defenders and me.

FIFA is not just a video game about soccer. At one level, it is a game that teaches players to read and decode how computers make decisions dynamically in the face of an open but constrained world defined by rules. *FIFA* is a game about learning what the AI does, how it does it, and collaborating with it. In *FIFA*, computational and human agents have to work together in order to win. The player needs to read the AI the same way as the AI is reading the player to make the statistically appropriate decision. The pleasure of playing *FIFA* is the pleasure of cooperation with the agency of software at the interface. Play acts here as a way of familiarizing us with the possibilities of AI, both in what it can do and what we can do with it, together.

Video games are relatively straightforward examples of interfaces, since they are technologies created to make worlds with their own rules, interactive processes, and spaces for agency. That's why it is productive to look for play elsewhere. There are examples of software that is not a video game and yet can only be experienced through play. For example, Vectorpark's *Feed the Head* is a digital toy that uses some video game structures and some interactive storytelling cues to allow us to engage with whimsical playful experiences.[28] It presents the player with a digital, interactive head that reacts to input in ways that are almost impossible to predict. The head opens up, the eyes roll back and are spit out, the nose falls and grows and becomes a cannon or a flying device.

Playing (with) *Feed the Head* is exploring the limits and possibilities of a software simulation. In fact, most interactions with playable and gameful software can be described as an exploration of the expressive possibilities of software while drawing a map of what the software allows or disallows. In the case of *Feed the Head,* that exploration is toyful and driven by the aesthetic pleasures of play. In the interface, where we meet this bizarre software agency, we have fun because this is meaningfully useless software. The impossible events that we trigger, the way this digital head reacts to our input, establish a way of exploring and making sense of what software does. We laugh, we approach the head with curiosity, we travel to its world to make sense of it, and in doing so, we are also making sense of who we can be, how we can act, in this particular interface.

These examples show how players can meet the agencies of software in the context of video games and toyful experiences. It is now time to take one step back and start a search for alien agency beyond games and toys.

Loving the Alien

In the information age, software is an agent: it does things to us, for us, with us, to the world, for the world. Computers act, people adapt to that action, and vice versa. Biological and artificial agency meet and entangle at an interface. In the case of video games and playable media, that interface is designed to facilitate the activity of playing with an artificial agent.

What toys and video games do for software agency is eliminate or contain ambiguity. In a well-designed video game, we know what we have to do, and we are given tools to learn to see what the software will do to and with us. Video games teach us to see and entangle with software agency, shaping human agency so no actions are ambiguous: almost everything a player does has somehow been encoded in the agency of the software. The interface in video games and software toys results in a minimization of ambiguity: video games tells us what we can do, what we cannot do, and why we should do it. One of the pleasures of playing these games is that they are unambiguous software agents in a clear and explicit way.

Software has a complicated relation with ambiguity. Computers act without emotional memory, without hesitation, faster than what we can imagine. They remember everything they have been commanded to remember, and they never deviate from their instructions. Seeing a computer learn, act, make decisions, provide input, change state: that is the experience of the agency of computers. But an important element of their uncanny agency has to do with their rigid approach to biological agencies and the material world: whatever cannot be computed does not exist.[29] Whatever is ambiguous, difficult to categorize, needs to be weeded out of the world in which software agents interact with each other, and with us.

When a thermostat changes temperature, when the smart home system turns the light on when it "sees" you, when the headphone stops the music because it has been taken off the ear—these are all the actions of software agents. They all need clear, formalized representations of their environment in order to create a world to entangle with humans. Thermostats need sensors to measure temperature within ranges; headphones require ears with the right shapes. To avoid ambiguity, norms and standards are codified in the software, from bodies to temperatures to the right amount of debt. We dream of terraforming Mars, but what we have done is a similar process in our world: we have software-formed the world so that these agencies could meet us. We turned the world into an interface. Our lifeworld is the world of practices of interfaces with software agencies. Playing is a way of meeting with these agencies at the interface. We want the information age to be playful not just for fun's sake, but also because play helps eliminate ambiguities through rules, therefore facilitating the relations established between human and artificial agents.

In 2017, I bought an iPhone X, the first model that had face recognition as a way of unlocking the device. Face recognition is based on a series of computer program trained in large data sets so it can recognize patterns in data, producing a statistically accurate response: my phone can recognize my face with precision. This is a creepy, dystopian technology. The fact that a portable computer produced by a corporation has enough data to recognize my face without doubt should be cause for alarm. That interface breaks boundaries we didn't know we had and cannot explicitly formulate.

To appease this negative feeling, Apple released at the same time a playful way of engaging with this face-recognition camera: the Animojis, an emoji that acts as a mask of the user (figure 2.4). It can recognize facial features such as mouth, eyes, and eyebrows and animate them responding to the user's facial expressions. Animojis are toyful instruments for understanding what the frontal camera of the phone is doing. They are an expressive, inefficient software functionality made for exploring the possibilities of a particular technology. Animojis normalize portable cameras with face recognition through the appropriative rhetoric of play. And so a camera that can recognize you is less creepy because it is also a toy that allows you to play with it. The possible ambiguities that the software agent could face, from our reluctance to have our face

Figure 2.4
The author as Animoji. Author's screenshot.

scanned to the position of the phone to have the face registered, are addressed through a playful design.

Animojis as interfaces are examples of how play is used to facilitate the entanglement with a modality of software agency that has questionable ethical and political implications. The interface is a vantage point from which we can observe these worlds. Politics, ethics, culture: they all take place not in the machines, or in the people, or in the computer programs, but where machines and people and programs meet and relate to each other and become entangled. There is no ethics of the information age outside of the interface because that's where agency is negotiated. The politics and economics of the information age will be the politics and economics of the interface. The interface is the place for relating human and software agencies, the place where these relations can be proposed, opposed, imposed, and configured. In the interface, culture finds new materials, new voices, new intersections of what can, should, or ought not to be expressed. The interface is the space of possibility of the information age, carved by relations among multiple agencies.

From the perspective of what happens to human agents when we are the point of the interface, we should think about practices: the things we do to stay in that interface, the specific actions and practices that lead us to have a world experience with(in) the interface. And that is why we need to look at play—because playing is a practice at the interface.

The Play Interface

The interface is where we meet alien agencies and become entangled with them. That meeting can take many forms—it is an experience of entanglement with the agency of software, and as such it can be defined by how it develops into a practice. For example, some of these interfaces are social. We use computational systems to satisfy social needs—to stay in touch, to greet, to be together. The entanglement with software agencies is determined by social goals. And thus the practices in that interface are defined by social purposes and social goals and reinforced by the design of those systems.

We also have work interfaces, like the one I am engaged with right now as I write these words, with multiple screens, programs, and networks helping me figure out how to describe precisely the way I am entangled with it. We have social interfaces, like Twitter or Instagram—agents designed to help us streamline the complications of presenting ourselves to others through screen-based systems.

There is also a play interface, in which the meeting of agencies is defined by playing. Probably Not creates a world in which the rules of the software that recognizes objects are entangled with the arbitrary rules of ridiculous software. Using it means learning to see the world like a silly computer system, but also understanding the world created by these processes—understanding what makes an object "recognizable" by an algorithm and what things these programs "see" in objects in order to categorize them. Probably Not shows what happens when we meet a software agency designed to play.

The play interface is defined by an entanglement of human and software agencies bound to rules and processes designed to be played. By playing, some of the rules of software become explicit; they become visible and shape the agency of both the human and the software together. Probably Not lets us take pictures to know what things are not. The play interface is the meeting point where we meet the agency of software.

This play interface also helps normalize forms of software agencies. A mobile phone with facial recognition capacities can identify the unique elements in our faces and store them in their proprietary machinery. This should be considered dystopian, a serious concern for privacy-minded people. But when presented as an Animoji, this very system is met in a different way: by playing. Facial recognition becomes software we can play with, software we meet not in the interface of surveillance or data extraction but in the play interface, where we can toy around with what the software can do. Is this world traveling? Is this meeting other agents lovingly? Or, in other words, are the interests of a corporation like Facebook when they allow playful filters for their Messenger or Instagram services? Or why does Apple or Google add humor to their voice assistant services? Surely to make things fun, but also to let us meet these systems of data extraction in a different context, as a form of playing. Maybe these playful applications of software are camouflaging under their fun the processes that reduce us to commercially valuable data. And we do so voluntarily because we like to play.

The play interface is a significant change in the way humans have played. Software always has rules, always has processes, always creates worlds. Engaging with software, meeting at an interface, is always becoming a part of the world created by software. Play is a way of configuring that interface, a tactic toward the world that is presented to us. Play allows for the submission or resistance to the rules and processes of software. Play opens up these worlds to pleasure, to laughter, to emotions, to fun. Playing software can be good. At the same time, play interfaces can present forms of control and engagement that can have negative implications. Play is about the imagination of potential possible relations, about the instantiation of those possibilities, and about the transformation of existing worlds into possible worlds. When the play interface uses humans not as agents but as mere data to be fed to software, we find a novel form of the corruption of play that Caillois argued happened when "reality" entered the domain of play.[30]

While I have an innate optimism and a romantic approach to play, the play interface is not only positive. Playing is often used as a way of facilitating and easing forms of control and exploitation. Playing software can be easing us into surrendering our agency to what can be computable by the politics and economics of automated systems. Playing creates potential new relations between human and artificial agents, but what we do to create those relations and to sustain them through play is still the domain of ethical thinking.

Software often presents itself as infallible as true, as long as we abide by its rules. But in the play interface, those rules can be bent, they can be negotiated, or they can be made into pleasurable determinism—we still have to do as we are told, but it can be fun. In most interfaces, human agency is reduced by the inflexible requirements of software: we write the way Microsoft Word wants us to write. In an ethically sustainable play interface, it is possible to modulate the agency of software, to downplay its system authority, to focus on the ambiguities left by the rules rather than in the clockwork precision of their processes. We can use object recognition to tell us what things are not. In the play interface, it is also possible to accept the pleasures of being controlled by software, diluting critical thinking for the sake of fun. Most play interfaces oscillate between both: the pleasure of being controlled and the pleasure of gaining control.

In *Play Matters* I wrote that play humanizes software. But that is not totally true. The play interface can also take place in a dangerous political position, in which the promises of play are used to facilitate being controlled by software agencies. Play can seduce us, and it can be weaponized to entertain us. As Neil Postman wrote in *Amusing Ourselves to Death*,[31] we live not in the age of Orwell's *1984* but in that of Huxley's *Brave New World*. Technology wants to entertain us so we don't see the extension of its agency, so we don't see how it turns everything into products and commodities, how play becomes another form of extractive, exploitative labor. The play interface can be corrupted; it can isolate us, and it can commodify us.

The play interface is not negative or positive: it is a particular configuration of the relation with software. If we want to understand the culture, ethics, and politics of the software age, we need to understand the play interface and what happens to things and agents at that meeting point.

3 Playthings

What happens when we meet the agency of software? Historically speaking, we play with it. Computers are obviously used for many other things than playing. But the role of play in the development of software cannot be understated. From Turing using the concept of games as a way of thinking about artificial intelligence, to Weizenbaum's role-playing-like ELIZA, software has been theorized, developed, and used as a thing that can be played with. The history of digital technologies is one of expanding forms of play, from video games to playful online cultures to digital toys. This expansion of results in an exploration of the limits of concepts such as "game," "toy," or "video game." The more we play with software, the more we blur boundaries of those concepts, making it difficult to see when playful interactions end and software toys start. There are more things we play with than what those categories describe, especially in the world of software. And even categories like "game" have suffered metamorphosis to cope with new phenomena like video games.

In this chapter, I introduce the concept of *plaything* to make sense of what happens to things and people when playing software. There are more things we play with than categories that properly define them. Trying to categorize every play-driven interaction with software using the category of game, video game, or toy can be misleading. Not every form of playable software is a game or a toy. Therefore, I propose the concept of plaything, understood as the materially based entanglement of agencies that takes place when playing.

Playthings are situated culturally, socially, politically, and economically, through concepts such as "games," "video games," "toys," or "playable media." For example, "video game" describes what a particular society understands as a particular type of software designed to be played with at a particular point in time. "Video game" is a category that situates a plaything in a social, cultural, and economic context. With the concept of plaything, I propose a way of applying play theory to software beyond "video games" or "toys."

I first published these ideas in "Playthings," an article published in the journal *Games and Culture.*[1] The article lays out the theoretical foundations of my argument, but it is a flawed argument. Game scholars Alex M. Layne and Cody J. Reimer pointed out in their podcast *Game Studies Review* how my theoretical concept of plaything needed to be explicitly connected to the feminist projects that inform my understanding of materialism. They also correctly suggested that writing about playthings required consideration of the negative connotation of the word, as a term of objectification, as well as its meaning related to sex toys. In this chapter, I present a revised version of this concept of playthings that can be used as a critical tool to understand the negative elements of playing software. I start by situating this concept in an academic tradition.

Theoretical Background

The concept of plaything draws heavily on new materialist philosophy as a bridge to the material aspect of play with its capacity to create subjectivities and new forms of being.[2] Game studies has recently witnessed an interest in this philosophy, particularly applying it to unconventional forms of play, such as speed running, ambient games, and AI-driven experiences.[3] The relation between play and materiality, including the materiality of software, is a topic that both Giddings and Simon addressed, applying concepts from media studies and sociology to understand what happens to things when we play with them.[4] These works provide insights into different material configurations of the practices of play and how they expand what kind of things we play with.

Jayemanne and Apperley called this interest in the material aspect of play a "material turn in game studies."[5] Game studies has slowly shifted toward an acknowledgment of the material conditions of production and consumption of games. Inspired by this work, I propose a concept that allows thinking about agency and materiality in the interface between software and humans. This chapter is an acknowledgment of the importance of this materialistic turn in game studies and my own contribution to it.

My appropriation of the word *plaything* is, like all other academic reinventions of a word, moderately risky. Dictionaries inform me that *plaything* is a synonym for *toy*, and Eugene Fink already used the concept to try to grasp every thing that would be part of the activity of play.[6] I have also learned that there is a negative connotation of the word that cannot be ignored: playthings can also be used as a derogative term usually applied to women. And playthings can also refer to sex toys. I propose playthings as a concept that embraces all of these meanings to signify the complexity of play as a cultural phenomenon. Beyond categorizing the things we play with, *playthings* explains the process of playing, what happens to any thing when and while it is part of playing, as well as its negative and positive relations to bodies. The other advantage of using this word is that it allows thinking about "games," "toys," and "playgrounds" as cultural concepts.

In the years it took to write this book, artificial intelligence became a dominant topic in academia and in society. Because of its explicit agency, in this chapter I use AI-based playthings as examples. When I write about AI, my ideas are inspired by the playful crafting projects of Gillian Smith, as well as by Julian Togelius's research on making playful things with computers, both using computers and together with computers.[7] Researchers working with AI know well that software is a plaything, in which the fun is to explore what software can do and what it does to us.

My use of the concept of plaything draws from a tradition of feminist thinkers who situated the body, especially the nonmale and nonnormative body, at the center of the possibilities and dangers of technology. To think about playthings and materiality is also to decenter the importance of the fixed dualistic categories and to understand that things are always in the making. *Playthings* wants to reflect how traditional categories that qualify the things we play with, like games or toys, are concepts that wield power and can be used to draw boundaries as to who gets to play. Playthings, understood as the ontological result of playing with things, could be a useful concept to engage with the tapestry of beings, agency, and play without falling into classifications and categorizations that can be used to perpetuate forms of exclusion. Playthings is, however, the most philosophical and abstract of the ideas presented so far. Let me start with an example of how *plaything* helps situate play practices with software in broader perspectives.

AI Is a (Play)Thing

In November 2016 I became infatuated with *Quick, Draw!* a quirky browser-based video game that challenges players to draw a doodle of a thing to see if the computer recognizes what it is. I was impressed by how the software could "see" castles and carrots and scorpions and whales. On the surface, *Quick, Draw!* is a competitive, skill-based (video)game. It has rules and a winning condition, and it is possible to get better at it. It is very much a video game that can only be played with a computer, as it is based on interacting with a deep learning system trained to recognize doodles. But reducing *Quick, Draw!* to just being a "video game" can be limiting.

Google, the developer of *Quick, Draw!*, is interested in more than just letting people enjoy their tools. Each doodle is an element in what is now "the largest doodling data set in the world" (https://quickdraw.withgoogle.com/data). As I will argue in chapter 6, *Quick, Draw!* turns players into workers who provide quality data points for the training of the machine learning algorithms owned by a corporation.

Mary L. Gray and Siddharth Suri described this work as "ghost work," "the human labor powering many mobile phone apps, websites, and artificial intelligence systems [that can be] hard to see—in fact, it's often intentionally hidden.[8] *Quick, Draw!* is a form of ghost play: an instrumentalization of the pleasures and benefits of play for the sake of improving the quality of AI systems. As I will argue in chapter 6, we have to situate play in the socioeconomic conditions in which it takes place. But before addressing that topic, I need to take a step back and think about what kind of thing *Quick, Draw!* is, so it is easier to understand why it is both a playable experience and an instrument for platform capitalism.[9]

I start with the core mechanic of the game. Doodling is a playful activity: a freeform type of drawing driven by exploration, curiosity, and skill. It is difficult to doodle "wrong"—it is an activity that does not quantify its results. Doodling keeps us entertained when lectures are boring, when meetings are too long, when train commutes become less of a novelty. In those contexts, we put our minds in creative idle mode, and doodles appear on paper.

The playfulness of doodling makes it an attractive interface for Google's data mining and technology-showcasing efforts. Machine learning algorithms need good-quality data sets to be more efficient, since they are built on statistical repetition of patterns based on historic data.[10] The larger and "cleaner" the data set, the better. For a computer to recognize what a doodle represents, it needs a large data set. If users get to produce those data as part of playing a video game, the algorithms have more and better data points to perform their predictions. And all of us "enjoy" this labor.

Producing data so that a computer can act on it is tedious. It consists on the repetitive tagging of visual data (photographs, doodles) with a preset list of categories. Ghost work of this kind is particularly demeaning because it consists almost exclusively on completing captchas, those small puzzle-like activities that are used to make sure that you are not a robot when accessing a website.[11] That's exactly what training data sets for machine learning consists of, and that's the why *Quick, Draw!* is an interesting example to understand the use of play in making technology more relatable. Through the lens of a game-like experience, we pleasurably test and train algorithms.

This is where the concept of plaything becomes relevant. *Quick, Draw!* is a plaything, that is, software that entangles with humans in a play interface. It has been designed to be played, to be fun, to provide pleasure while engaging with its deep learning system. It is presented to us as a game. *Quick, Draw!* is a plaything presented under the frame of being a "video game," so we can situate it in a specific social, cultural, economic, and political context.

If Google itself calls *Quick, Draw!* a "game," why do we need the concept of plaything? *Quick, Draw!* is a point of contact between a machine learning system that has a certain agency and humans who interact with it. In that point of contact, a new, small, contained world comes to being—that of *Quick, Draw!* Making sense of that world implies understanding the agency of the machine learning system. The cultural concept of "video game" helps structure that playful activity. Because this plaything is interpreted as a video game, its rules and mechanics are situated in the cultural, social, and economic context of games and gaming, even if playing with this thing is actually a form of training an algorithm. *Quick, Draw!* is a plaything designed to make pleasurable the training of a machine learning system. This plaything is experienced through the cultural lens of the concept "video game."

Defining *Quick, Draw!* as a game obscures the role it has in the economics of platform capitalism. By calling it a game, Google wants to make training data sets "fun," normalizing playing software as a way of providing data or training data sets. Using the concept of game implies drawing on its cultural meaning. It's not training; it's "just a game," a thing that is only for fun, not productive. AI is a thing we can play with. But how did it get there? It's time to go back to world traveling and relationality.

Relationality and the World

Playing as world traveling is a relational mode of engaging with software. In the interface as point of encounter, playing is relating to the agency of software. These relations seek pleasure though the exploration of boundaries and rules. In the meeting point of the interface, something happens to the things that are playing. Playing does something to the bodies and materials at play.

The body is often an instrument or recipient of the pleasures of playing: feeling how a ball bounces and the tactile proximity of other bodies in Twister are sources of fun. At the same time, our body relates to materiality in play by exploring the properties of objects as they can contribute to embodied pleasure. A properly pumped basketball or football is more fun to play with than a flat one. The satisfying sound and vibrations of a tennis racket make returning a good shot even better.

When thinking about software, we sometimes can forget about the fact that the body is also there, experiencing the agency of computers in the interface. We also tend to forget that all software is material, based on machines performing calculations, subject to the laws of physics, exuding heat and consuming electricity. Interacting with software is relating to computational systems; playing software involves the body in that experience, and highlights the materiality of software.

The small things that make interactions with software feel different, like pulling down to refresh a news feed, are simulations of physical properties. For example, when I'm reading the newsfeed on my mobile phone app for Twitter, pulling down to refresh actually feels like pulling down: there's a resistance at some point that makes me feel that I have reached a physical end (of a scroll, maybe?). Suddenly, sending a fetch request to a server feels like pulling a material thing.

Simulations of physics like this help make interaction more embodied. They also open up for playful activities. Another way of interpreting the pull-down-to-refresh mechanic is as an instantiation of a slot machine–inspired invocation of chance. Maybe I will get lucky after this pull and will read something interesting. Otherwise I can keep on trying my luck. This is not exclusive of mobile phone software: when I move my physical mouse around very fast, the pointer increases in size, a comfortable usability feature that is also playful. The way program windows minimize themselves by shrinking or the pulsating insistence of my phone when it gets a new email is a reminder that software is experienced by a body, that at the interface there is an embodied, material meeting of agencies. These small, designed interactions allow a noninstrumental, nonefficient relationship with software. They are also suggestions that can inspire us to play with software.

If we wanted to read data from servers, the proper, efficient way would probably involve as few interactions as possible that are as clear as they can possibly be. We would end up with something like the control panel of a nuclear power station: useful, usable, efficient, and boring. But pull-to-refresh, or shake-to-undo, or physics-based scrolling speeds are more than just functional. They are aesthetic, and they can be used not just to fulfill a function but also to pass time, to tinker around, to fidget. They are openings to play because there is more to them than just function.

When software goes beyond functional, play can take over. An element of surprise, a little expression in the form of a shake of a particular embodied feel that might not be expected, can quickly become an invitation to playing software. Using gifs and emoticons, and creating infinite space and infinite worlds in a computer simulation are all appropriations of software that have an element of play. These software systems are not games or toys—at least not exactly. They are things we can play with.

Allison Parrish's *Nonsense Laboratory*, another Google commission like *Quick, Draw!*, uses machine learning to let users play with words.[12] It's not exactly a game, but a collection of playable engagements with language mediated by a computer system trained with different language models. It is not a game, it may be a toy, but it certainly is a plaything: a way of playing with language and with an AI. It's even less directed and more whimsical than *Quick, Draw!* Its purpose is more to have fun, to be surprised, to play with language together with an AI. It is establishing a relation with software by playing with it and together with it.

Is *Nonsense Laboratory* a game? Or is it a toy? Actually why does it matter? It is certainly a piece of software we can use to relate to AI through play. It could be seen as a game, but it is substantially different from any other games. Maybe game scholars like Stephanie Boluk and Patrick LeMieux would call it a video game, software designed to be played with that is different from the traditional category of games. These words help us describe some characteristics of *Nonsense Laboratory* while also missing out on others. What kind of work are we doing when we call something we play with a game, a video game, or a toy? These are cultural and historical categories, fraught with the scars of multiple culture wars. In their book *Real Games*, Mia Consalvo and Chris Paul discuss how some games are not considered by parts of the community of players to be "real games."[13] The concept of game has been used as an exclusionary boundary by vocal minorities supported by corporations, a way of drawing a line on what and who is accepted in a culture and who is not. By challenging the notion of "real games" and investigating the origins of this phrasing, Consalvo and Paul illustrate how the concept of game is a cultural one.

Thinking about play as a relational mode of engaging with technology implies moving beyond these cultural categories. It is also important to have a concept that accounts for all the things in the world people play with that are not games or toys—all the things that become temporary materials for play. It is also important to have a concept that highlights how games and toys are contextual to a culture at a particular point in time. The things we play with are described and defined by cultural concepts, but they have a different nature. And there are more things we play with than just games or toys. Only a limited amount of software is made to be a game, but almost all software is open to being played with. Play is more than human action changing the world; it is also things changing themselves. In the act of play, software becomes a plaything.

Thinking about Things

We like to think about things as relatively static, knowable entities. The book you're holding is a book, the chair is a chair, and so on. One of my life's most fascinating cultural shocks happened when I moved to the United States and realized how packed with *stuff* that country is, how much it is a country of *things*. Go into a store, and there will be shelves upon shelves of things, surrounding you, creating a landscape of absurd capitalist mundanity. For affluent

Westerners, the world is often an accumulation of things to contemplate, desire, interact with, own, break, and rarely mend. But not all things are the same: some hold emotional value, some have meaning beyond their functionality, some are the origin of affect and emotional responses. We don't just live surrounded by things: we relate to them. If we want to understand play, we need to understand it as one such relational engagement with things.

This material approach to play starts with the premise that there is a difference between objects and things.[14] As a starting point, let's consider objects as the stuff in the world before we interact with them. Objects are static materials. They have properties we can describe. A door that hasn't been opened, the computer that's powered off, the TV screen or the car or even the mighty taco: they are all objects around us.

The second premise is that the concept of things describes active materials, the result of agents interacting with objects.[15] An object that is interacted with becomes a thing. A good way of grasping this distinction is that we can use adjectives when we talk about things. The chair becomes comfortable or uncomfortable when someone sits on it. The car becomes a lemon that won't turn on when needed. The delayed kitchen clock, never on time, will make us arrive late. Things are active: they entangle us; they shape and are shaped by our actions, emotions, and intentions. Things *do* stuff.[16] A door allows us to have private conversations. The computer allows me to type these words. The screen distracts me. Things *act*. Objects are passive; things can have agency, they can act on us, on themselves, on their surroundings. And in that process, they are configured and reconfigured; they become some*thing*, shaped by as well as shaping human agency.[17]

In the interface, software becomes a thing. The software I am writing this book with is only a thing; it is only acting in that meeting of agencies. The way this software lays out the page, structures the view of the different documents that form this book in folders and subfolders and individual chapters: all of these possibilities are actions that help determine how I write and how I think (figure 3.1). When I want to write this book, the software object of my word-processing program becomes a thing at the point of the interface, mixing its agency with my own agency. I am not the writer of this book. This book is written by me-and-this-software, a meeting of agencies in an interface from which a thing, a human–computer hybrid, emerges.[18]

Computational things emerge in the practices of human agency negotiating software agency. A lot of *things* in our material, physical world can be playthings. The humble stick, an inductee in the Toy Hall of Fame, is a plaything that can help in infinite forms of play. A pen we fidget with while waiting for a call is a plaything,

This material approach to play starts with the premise that there is a difference between objects and things (Ingold, 2010, 2012). As a starting point, let's consider objects as the stuff in the world, before we interact with it. Objects are static materials. They have properties we can describe. A door that hasn't been opened, the computer that's powered off, the TV screen or the car or even the mighty taco, they are all objects around us.

The second premise is that the concept of things describes active materials, the result of agents interacting with objects (Ingold, 2012). An object that is interacted with becomes a thing. A good way of grasping this distinction is that we can use adjectives when we talk about things. The chair becomes comfortable or uncomfortable when someone seats on it. The car becomes a lemon that won't turn on when needed. The delayed kitchen clock, never on time, will make us arrive late. Things are active, they entangle with us, they shape and are shaped by our actions, emotions, and intentions. Things *do* stuff (Verbeek, 2005). A door allows us to have private conversations. The computer allows me to type these words. The screen distracts me. Things *act*. Objects are passive; things can have agency, they can act on us, on themselves, on their surroundings. And in that process, they are configured and re-configured, they become some*thing*, shaped by as well as shaping human agency (Frauenberger, 2019; Introna, 2014).

In the interface, software becomes a *thing*. The software I am writing this program with is only a *thing*, it is only acting, in that meeting of agencies. The way this software lays out the page, structures the view of the different documents that conform this book in folders and subfolders and individual chapters, all of these possibilities are actions that help determine how I write, and how I think. When I want to write this book, the software object of my word-processing program becomes a thing, at the point of the interface, mixing its agency with my own agency. I am not the writer of this book. This book is written by me-and-this-software, a meeting of agencies in an interface from which a thing, a human-computer hybrid, emerges (Barad, 2007; D. Haraway, 2016).

Figure 3.1
This page, captured twice. Author's screenshot.

challenging us to keep it balanced with our fingers. But there is also software we can play with—not just "video games" but also digital camera filters, user interface elements, voice assistants, text generators, machine learning systems. What we do with the stick when we play is the same as what we do with Alexa when we try to make it swear, or to software when we force it to do what is not functional or usable: we relate to it by playing. In doing so, it becomes a plaything.

Things We Play With

Things mediate our being in the world; they are the point of contact between human and nonhuman agency, between bodies and materials. When objects become things, they become shaped by their materiality but also by the actions they take and facilitate, the world and experiences they mediate, and the intentions and actions of whomever uses them. The thing that emerges in play is a *plaything*—an arrangement of materials, bodies, and agencies defined by the relational activity of play. Playthings emerge when we play with objects.

The concept of plaything is a way of explaining things from the perspective of relational play. Consider, for example, Apple's fluid interfaces with design vocabulary.[19] When introducing iOS 12, Apple also introduced a new vocabulary for their visual interfaces. This vocabulary makes use of physical simulations for the design of user interface elements such as tables, boxes, labels, and buttons. Taken to its extreme, the liquid interfaces with vocabulary can turn almost any user interface element into a physics object with mass and velocity. Labels, tables, text: they can all behave like simulated physical objects. Why? First, so the body becomes involved in the interaction with software. We feel the weight of fluid interfaces, their velocity, their elasticity. And in doing so, the interaction with a mundane visual interface element becomes a source of surprise, a revelation of agency that suggests playful world traveling. Using software becomes fun beyond the functional.

By connecting standard computational visual elements with a physics engine, Apple opens up for the pleasurable exploration of the interactions allowed by the software. Visual interface elements become toys that can be dragged, pulled, and thrown; software agency becomes a plaything that rewards the exploration of rules and processes. These explorations of possibilities do not punish experimentation and failure, and thus are encouraging ways of learning and becoming emotionally attached to the software products we are encouraged to consume.

Playthings are not "games," or "toys," or "playgrounds." "Games" is a cultural category that encompasses specific types of playthings. "Toys" is another of those categories. A plaything is a thing that comes into being by playing; it is materials put in motion by play. A video game, the toys from our childhood, the rubber band that we fiddle with, the pull-to-refresh user interface that so satisfyingly bounces back: these are all playthings, coming to being when we play.

Not all software, hardware, or objects can become playthings. Some technologies with agency in the world have been designed to resist becoming a plaything. The hardware and software in nuclear reactors or in airplane cockpits is designed with redundancies and backstops so the operators and pilots do not turn these devices into playthings. This is not to say that ultimately they cannot force play into these systems, but these systems are designed to actively resist becoming a plaything. Part of the task of designers and developers of technology resides in thinking about how much the technological systems and agencies can resist or submit to becoming playthings. The duty of a play designer is to investigate, and design for, the evident possibilities of objects to become playthings, opening them to interpretation and experience through the lens of play.

With the concept of playthings, I want to move away from understanding play as the imposition of human agency in the world. Playing in the information age is negotiating agencies with software. It goes beyond "using" things to mediate human agency in the world. Playing is creating playthings that mediate the entanglement between human and artificial agency

Playing helps us make sense of what software is and what it can do for us and with us. Sometimes we will see these playthings as games—structured activities with goals and purposes and quantifiable development of skills, as in video games and in motion trackers. Playthings as games can also be landscapes of exploration of personality and possible configurations of who we are, as in role-playing digital games or in social media. Sometimes these playthings are toys, open-ended vehicles for co-creative exploration of expressive and pleasurable possibilities. For example, using image filters on social media makes computer-mediated communication more playful. But no matter how we place them in culture, they are playthings—things with agency we meet at an interface created by playing.

When a thing is created by play, it becomes a structure of rules, processes, and agencies that meet in material and embodied circumstances. This entanglement is characterized by expression, pleasure, appropriation, and the possibility to negotiate agency. The age of computational play can be defined by the emergence of a new type of plaything: the software plaything, created by human play as much as it creates (new forms of) human play.

Software as Plaything

One of the courses I teach focuses on developing playful experiences with different software tools. Every semester I try to select tools that have relatively poor uses outside very specific situations and encourage my students to play with them. Some of my favorite examples from that class were augmented reality applications that allowed people to go fishing anywhere, virtual reality simulators of spaceships controlled by voice, and a piece of AI-powered software that would help users know the gender of bread.

Perhaps my favorite software to play with in that class is speech recognition and synthesis. As part of the learning process for the course, I recommend that students check out the wonderful Mozilla tutorials on browser-based speech synthesis. One of the examples in this tutorial consists of a humble text box in which users can type text so that they can listen to the different voices and accents available in the system. That very simple interaction is open for a playful appropriation. Throughout the years, I have seen people input bizarre words to see how the system pronounces them or try to fool the system into saying obscenities by mispronouncing words in other languages. Others have tried to create beat boxes or to read stories out loud. What this tutorial does is more than just show how to access Web-based speech recognition and synthesis. The tutorial fosters a playful approach to making sense of how we can talk to a browser and have it understand what we are saying.

Through the exploration and creation of new boundaries and new relations between the user and an artificial agent, software becomes a plaything. Relating to software agency opens a constellation of possibilities, a modulation of agencies united in the purpose of the pleasurable exploration of boundaries through surprise, curiosity, and imagination. By playing, we identify and establish relations with the rules and processes that constitute software. These relations are based on the will of challenging their rules or submitting to them for the convenient pleasures they deliver. In that process, something happens to both the user/player and the software. We learn to use software by trying out things. We learn about expressive new possibilities of software by toying around with them.

This is not necessarily a happy, positive, creative activity. Playthings are not necessarily good things. You think that something you play with, say, a toy, would never spy on you, or steal your data, or surveil you because it is a harmless, moderately irrelevant, "playful" thing. Until it is not. If we take speech processing and turn it into a plaything, and then we situate that in the body of a doll, we will end up with Mattel's Hello Barbie, a creepy toy connected to a speech recognition server that is constantly listening to children while they play to more accurately market to their "needs."

Or what about using machine vision playfully, allowing software to transform your face based on the elements it recognizes? It is certainly turning software into a plaything, making us relate to machine vision through the useless, fun way it has of "seeing" our face and reacting to it—of course, until the playful transformations of your face in FaceApp are revealed to be another form of extracting biometric data from users.[20]

Playthings can be very serious software—fun experiences of systems that will extract data for commercial purposes, with programs that will measure and evaluate our performance and will control our actions and our bodies if we let them. As long as interacting with these systems feels like playing, the risks and concerns that the progressive digitization of society raises might be ignored. Playthings reward exploration and curiosity. At the same time, they can make it difficult to take seriously the world created by software and the limitations on human agency imposed by computer programs. The concept of playthings lets us see what happens to software when we play with it, and by decoupling play from the cultural concepts of "games" or "toys ," we can have a more critical understanding of how playthings are deployed in society.

Video games can give us an example of the applicability of this concept. Playable software like *Dear Esther* and *Firewatch* are essentially first-person perspective experiences of designed interactions with a three-dimensional world simulation, structured around dispersed narratives. When these video games were launched, a schism happened in the community of people (too) invested in these games: since these were interactive software without goals, skill progression, and other cultural markers of what we have historically called "games," a vocal part of the gaming community defined them as "not games." As Consalvo and Paul illustrate in their work on "real games, walking simulators challenged dominant conceptions around what makes video games "games."[21] In their work, they convincingly argue that this ownership of the concept of "game" and what can be categorized as such is also political: many of what the Right conservative wing of the gaming community considers not to be games are playthings created and played by minorities, from LGBTQ creators to people of color.[22] There is power in defining what a game is, and that power was initially wielded against those who aspired to expand the expressive and ethical palette of video games.

But people *played* walking simulators. Regardless of which initial category was used to describe this software, players understood these as playthings, interactive software designed to be played. Whether they are games or not has nothing to do with their intrinsic properties but with the place we want to give them in culture. In this case, walking simulators were trapped in a culture war in which the concept of games has been hostage for a long time. Following again Consalvo and Paul's arguments, calling "walking simulators" games is a cultural and political argument. Defining them as games (or as not games) situates this particular type of plaything within the cultural domain of games, potentially expanding and diversifying it. In 2021, it was not polemic to consider walking simulators as video games, an illustration of how the cultural concept of video game can always be expanded to encompass more types of playthings.

Walking simulators are software playthings, designed as interfaces that we relate to through play. When these playthings were released, it was difficult to classify them in our cultural norm of "video games" because even though they were playthings that showed similarity to video games, they lacked some characteristics of what was known as a video game. Time passed, people played with that software, and walking simulators became accepted culturally as games. They were always playthings, but it took time for culture to ascribe to them the label of game.

A similar thing is happening to toys. Smartphones are not toys. They are gadgets or gizmos.[23] Yet many of the interactions that are established with that particular machine are presented through the lens of play, from animated user interfaces to sassy voice assistants, Animojis, image filters, or animated backgrounds. Cell phones present themselves often as playthings so it becomes easier to understand what exactly they can be used for. We won't call them toys because "toy" is a cultural concept that typically encompasses the kind of playthings that are central to a child's experience of the world. Adults don't play with toys except when having sex. Adults play with "gadgets" because "gadgets" are culturally defined to be the appropriate plaything for adults to play with. Gadgets are not toys, but they often are playthings. That is the power of this concept: to be able to look at the role of play in shaping the relations of agencies, materials, and bodies without committing to cultural conflicting notions like "games," "toys," or "gadgets." At the same time, it allows us to see the use and evolution of concepts created in and by culture and societies to make sense of playthings.

There are of course other types of software toys that the concept of plaything encompasses. Software-driven sexual hardware is also a part of the information age—the field of teledildonics studies and develops sex toys that are enhanced by software. In fact, software-driven sex toys are perhaps the best example of playthings: these things act as material encasings for software agency that relates to human agency in the particular interface of a sexual encounter. Sex can be fun, it can be a form of play, and therefore it can also be a way of relating to the agency of software.[24] When we relate to what a sex toy can do, we're turning it into a plaything, whether in the way it vibrates or in the way it allows for remote lovers to stay close thanks to cloud-driven sex hardware, like the We-Vibe Sync vibrator. Thanks to that device, it is possible for couples to have sex remotely, with one partner controlling the vibrations of the device. That intercourse entangles two bodies and a material device controlled by software. There is no better definition of an interface in the context of this book than that of a remote-controlled vibrator. And in that interface, with bodies and software and materials deeply entangled with each other, a plaything emerges.

Digital sex toys are the perfect playthings: they highlight that the body is an inescapable part of human agency. They also make present material the agency of software, through rubber and silicone and actuators and haptics of many types, digital bodies relating to physical bodies.[25] And this relation happens in the play interface of sex, a space of possibility where the playful, loving exploration of other agencies is a sublime form of fun.

Sex can also bring us to the dark side of playthings. According to the *Cambridge Online Dictionary*, a plaything can also be understood as a person who is used "without respect and forced to do things for someone else's pleasure or advantage." *Plaything* can be a gendered derogatory term that involves a demeaning of an individual, a reduction of an agent to the role of mere servant to selfish pleasures. I retain this possible meaning in my understanding of plaything when it comes to software.

As I have said, software becomes a plaything when we play with it. But there is also the possibility of us, humans, becoming playthings in the meeting with the agency of software. When human agency is captured by a software system in play, but the purpose of the activity is not play but a predatory form of value extraction, then we become the playthings of software. The case of FaceApp is significant: by letting us tinker with the possibilities of image recognition, it feels like playing. But at the same time, we become things that software plays with in order to create a comprehensive database of faces that can be commercialized or exploited.

Similarly, the playful engagement with emotional reactions on social media can turn us into playthings. When we like or share a post, the algorithm will choose for us other posts that we can also like, a reinforcement loop that turns us into the plaything of recommendation algorithms. By proxy, we users also become the playthings of the platforms that control our playing with software.

When playing software, we should always question whether we are becoming playthings for software agents. The interface as meeting point of human and artificial agencies should also be the place to ask uncomfortable questions about who is playing, and why. If playing software is not a form of world traveling that allows us to lovingly meet the agency of software and to be met by it lovingly as well, then we are going to be playfully exploited. Our bodies become data points, our actions inputs for systems that process and quantize data for purposes we have not agreed on. Playing software is also about the ethics and politics of creating and interacting with playthings, especially when we become the playthings of software.

Adding a new concept to an already crowded landscape of theories is an act of academic cruelty. Yet here I am, and here is the concept of playthings. It is actually a useful one. As software permeates more of our lives and its agency becomes more entangled with ours, we are going to see new forms of play emerge. I am writing these words as text generators like GPT-3 are becoming darlings of the computer science and art communities. These are not just tools, instruments to further human knowledge or solve specific problems. AI and other forms of explicit software agency are best understood by playing with them, because when they become playthings, we are able to trace the boundaries of their possibility space and formulate new ways of conceiving what they can do in and to the world. Breaking software a bit, twisting it, teasing it to extract the unexpected—all of these are forms of playing with software or making it into a plaything. And it is not doing so because they are games, video games, or toys. It's doing so because playing software is making sense of software, and making sense of software is creating playthings.

4
Personalities

This chapter starts with a challenge: take a piece of paper and a pencil, close your eyes, and draw Alexa—not the pucky piece of hardware that is hopefully not sitting somewhere in your home, but *Alexa*. Give it a body, any body. Is it an octopod? Humanoid? How many mouths does it have? If you're a role player, let me up the challenge. Take a character sheet from any game you like, *Call of Cthulhu* or *Dungeons and Dragons*, for example, and make a character sheet for Siri. What are its attributes? What are its flaws? How do you imagine these assistants to be? And when you've done this exercise, it's time to reflect: Where does that image come from?

Of all the technologies that have succeeded in the information age, voice assistants like Siri and Alexa are the most fascinating to me. As a play and games scholar, I find video games interesting because they are asserting themselves as a dominant cultural form. But I think voice assistants are symptomatic of a capital change in play culture, driven by computational media. Reflecting *through* voice assistants, in this chapter I argue that the dominant form of play in the information age is make-believe. In *Play and the Human Condition*, Henricks suggests that "contemporary players are *performative* selves."[1] Drawing on that observation, as well as on Kendall

Walton's theory of make-believe at the root of aesthetic experience, I propose that the agential role of software in shaping the information age is slowly shifting the dominant form of play from agonistic play to make-believe.[2]

This raises an interesting issue, as Lugones's theory of play, the foundation of this book, explicitly calls out a particular form of make-believe: "In role-playing, the person who is a participant in the game has a *fixed conception of him or herself.*"[3] I disagree with Lugones's understanding of role playing. Make-believe is a form of world traveling, perhaps *the* paradigmatic form of world traveling, because it is not about having a fixed conception of the self but about becoming another. The characters we play, the roles we take show that the self is never fixed; it is always traveling toward others and other worlds. It is not surprising that some of the most influential theories of games and play of the 2010s, like Jaakko Stenros's or Sebastian Deterding's, build on Goffmanian approaches.[4] Goffman understood how our selves are also presentations toward others and the role of fun and play in the practice of the everyday self.[5] Make-believe is essential to the information age because it is the process of creating and practicing subjectivities that entangle with artificial agency.

I don't want to downplay the importance of competitive play. Many of the positive and negative sides of playing software are the outcome of using computers in computing human behaviors in competitive framings. For example, the quantification of communication and socialization in social media drives the economics and culture of these networks.[6] Similarly, the stubborn commercial dominance of competitive video games illustrates how agonistic play is still central to game-like experiences. For a vast majority of people, thinking about video games is thinking about the propagandistic playgrounds of conflict in the medals of duty or calls of honor that top the sales charts year after year. Those are principally agonistic games in which players can pretend to be the heroes of militaristic empires.

But changes are happening. For example, we can argue that social media from the perspective of play requires a form of make-believe, of creating and shaping who we are.[7] Social media foster the creation of a role-playing persona. Similarly, noncompetitive video games are becoming dominant, from the sprawling avant-garde narrative of *Kentucky Route Zero* to the wholesome world of *A Short Hike*,[8] world building as a form of game design based on make-believe is becoming a stronger cultural force. The importance of make-believe in aesthetics was central to Kendall Walton's *Mimesis as Make-Believe*, which in turn is the foundation of Grant Tavinor's *The Art of Videogames*.[9] These authors consolidated the importance of make-believe in aesthetics and in video games. I extend that argument to all forms of culture that derive from playing software. The attention paid to narrative and personality as the unique expressive means of computational media is the foundation of this paradigmatic shift.

Playing as a way of making sense of software is a practice of make-believe. By looking at the personalities and voices given to artificial agents, we have a vantage point to observe the use of play to engage with software and make sense of it and how artificial agencies become playthings. Drawing on media theory and human–computer interaction research, this chapter follows the voices of artificial agents as examples of the role of pretense in playing software.

A Question of Attitude

At home, Siri is always there. When I am cooking, it helps me with time. I don't need to look out the window to check the weather, and if I have a question about math or measuring units or the universe, Siri is there to help. Siri is also in my teaching, invoked as an example of the many faces of play. And thanks to the board game *Hey Robot*, Siri has also become a part of our playing family, even though it is not really that good at playing games.[10] Siri's voice is around my practices with technology in a subtle but persistent way.

In *Play Matters*, I wrote about Siri as an example of the way play can be used to create relations with technology. This chapter expands that observation. Siri has been designed with playful elements, presenting itself as having a personality, being opinionated, sporting a mischievous sense of humor. In *Play Matters*, I argued that this personality is an illustration of how play is an appropriative way of making personal the otherwise alien behavior of a phone that recognizes its user's voice and reacts to it. Play makes smartphones approachable, and it is a mode of making it easier to understand what a listening computer can do for you.

But what does this mean? This type of playful design was a strategy for Apple engineers to help make this new technology emotionally resonant. There is more to this adoption of personality than a clever design and commercial approach. It is not enough to say that "Siri is playful"; if playing creates worlds, what does Siri tell us about the world(s) of the information age?

Let's go back to the premise of this book: playing software is a way of relating to the alien agencies of software, traveling to creating new worlds in an entanglement of biological and artificial agencies. Make-believe is a strategy to make sense of the world. Without make-believe, these computational rules and processes could just be ignored or blindly obeyed. In the information age, we are numbers in spreadsheets, entries in data constructs, input providers. For humans and for animals, the information age can reduce us to the point of being just what can be calculated. That's why we play with software: to try to escape this inevitable reduction.

When we are playing software, processes and computational rules become play rules and play actions. They are perceived as something voluntarily accepted and fun. Without a certain attitude toward software, without a belief that the rules and processes of software are efficient and accurate and fair, our information age world would be one step closer to a mechanized dystopia, a global Amazon warehouse where everybody is routed and steered by planetary computational systems.

The world of software agents exists, but only inasmuch as we collectively decide that these are agents *doing things*. Living in this computational world is also wanting to live in this world, actively playing along by the rules that software puts in front of us. Computers that have personalities are symptomatic examples of what kind of make-believe is required for play to make sense of software.

Philosopher Bernard Suits wrote about play requiring a particular attitude to come into being.[11] Focusing on the study of games, Suits identified that players needed to accept rules in order to experience play. C. Thi Nguyen has taken this idea and explored it further in his work on games, agency, and aesthetics, situating that lusory attitude as a fundamental defining quality of games and, by extension, of certain forms of play.[12] The lusory attitude can also be used to explain the importance of make-believe in the context of playing in the information age.

Both playing and software create a world through rules and processes. Playing can make it fun to live in the boundaries created by software, but that possibility needs to be communicated to people somehow. Make-believe is a form of lusory attitude that facilitates the engaging with the rules of software as if they were rules of play. Gamification, for example, is often used in productivity software to facilitate the tracking of behavior and the development of new practices. It makes users think that professional networking, or the development of a particular skill, is like a game. The logic behind gamification is simple: if play is fun and we make work feel like a video game, then work will be fun. The implications of this argumentation are the focus of chapters 5 and 6. For now, I focus my attention on voice assistants.

The fact that many contemporary AI systems are presented as capable of playing is in itself an illustration of the role that make-believe has in facilitating the lusory attitude. Siri is an instrument in my household, a tool to measure time and get quick access to some information I can't be bother to type or tap for. But it is also a companion, a plaything I ask to tell jokes, a personality I look forward to explore when I am bored, because I pretend that it's *not* just a voice interface to a vast machinery of computational systems.

A form of lusory attitude takes command when I play software. This attitude uses make-believe to structure the entanglement with software agencies. I pretend Siri has a personality, and my interactions with it are not just transactional exchanges of information but personal connections. I relate to Siri through play, because I pretend it is *Siri*, and not just software. This attitude is central to a particular history of computing.

Tell Me How You Feel

It all begins with ELIZA, the patient and curious psychologist that Joseph Weizenbaum developed to illustrate the possibilities of natural language processing and early artificial intelligence. ELIZA was a revolutionary program: it allowed users to interact with a simulated psychologist that would appear to understand what they were typing and would reply in ways that suggest a limited, pretense-based version of therapy.

Weizenbaum developed ELIZA as an interactive thought experiment. The purpose of ELIZA was to illustrate what AI could do, how natural language processing would work, and explore the ways in which Turing's imitation game[13] could be put into practice.[14] Weizenbaum created ELIZA to show that computers could understand human language within limited domains and that a human, given a particular setting, might not be able to tell whether they are interacting with a computer or not, effectively passing the so-called Turing test.[15]

Voice assistants and ELIZA are not intelligent, but they seem to be so because they are entangled with us in constrained domains of interaction, like web browsing for shopping or porn consumption. In those contexts, they may seem "intelligent" because the context of those interactions informs what we expect from the interaction. This means that a bot with limited but relevant data about a context can provide responses that a human may interpret as intelligent. But it goes both ways: humans performing machinic tasks in certain contexts can pass as software. Sometimes when I am waiting in line for some services, I wonder if the voice at the other side of the phone is human, especially when the operator is reading from a script. When interacting with bureaucracy, I often wonder if the person at the other side of the desk is a replicant.

ELIZA was a paradoxical success. Weizenbaum recalls how people spent time talking to it *even if they knew* it was just software.[16] Pretense was too powerful: this computer was understanding what we said, and we wanted to tell it our secrets. Even now, when we have access to the vast machineries of Siri and Alexa, chatting with ELIZA is interesting because it listens to us, it takes care of us, it helps us. ELIZA is a case of play making sense of software.

Make-believe allows us to find patterns of action in how things operate. Pretending that ELIZA was a psychologist was a way of interpreting what we need to do. Pretending that a generative text engine like GPT-3 creates texts could be a way of understanding how we write. Make-believe is not necessarily about making things come to life, but about donning them with agency so that we can establish a negotiation of agencies. Make-believe is the foundational relational mode with many types of software.

Reeves and Nass documented this phenomenon in *The Media Equation*, empirically proving that we treat media as social agents.[17] But it's not just media: I talk to my computer and close its lid in specific ways so it goes to sleep because it is not a case of faulty wiring but a quirk of its personality. After a week in the cold mountains of

Norway, I found myself patting my car as if it was a pet, because it behaved well and the engine did start. A house I once lived in *conspired* against us by letting rain in. These *things* were acting, and I was pretending that their actions were intentional. In my world experience, these things were agents. There are many ways of understanding the agency of things in the world, but here I choose to observe it through the lens of play and make-believe, to observe the agencies that emerge when things *pretend* to have personalities.[18]

So although we know about how powerful make-believe is in shaping our engagement with things, we are still surprised that people reacted to ELIZA as if it was an actual psychologist. Ever since interacting with ELIZA or any of its descendants, many of us have enjoyed pretending that the computer understood us, that it knew what we were talking about, and that it reacted on it in a show of intelligence. ELIZA taught us to pretend that the computer could hear us, understand us.

Until computers actually started listening to us.

Voice-controlled, AI-powered assistants are the most recent iteration of the application of make-believe to interacting with computers. Siri is an interface, a point of encounter between human and computational agency. This interface is different because it makes use of advances in processing power, programming techniques, and sensor quality that make it possible for a computer to listen, understand, and react to human speech. But in essence, ELIZA and Siri are the same: a point of contact between human and computational agencies that require make-believe to become meaningful—and most of our interfaces become places of make-believe.

Pretending Software

Talking to a computer is basically providing instructions for software to perform processes. It is not significantly different from writing an instruction on the command line or double-clicking an icon on a graphical user interface. But voice brings into the experience more than just giving a command. Talking implies listening and establishing a relation between speaker and recipient, between who talks and who listens. The classic relation with a computer is that of providing commands and instructions to make it perform actions. Speaking, however, is a different approach. As a general trope in science fiction, the advanced AIs of spaceships are systems that are talked to and talk back. In speculative fiction, speaking to a technological device is typical of an artificial intelligence that is on level with human intelligence.

Talking to the computer is starting a conversation, connecting with it, relating to it. In *Play Matters*, I wrote about how Siri's programmed sense of humor was an example of playfulness. But is also something else: it is a part of the ritual of establishing a conversational relation with Siri. The amount of appropriative exploration that a classic computer interaction vocabulary allows for is limited: click, type, return. But speaking invokes a social practice that opens up for all the forms of playing with language and with conversation. Speaking to a computer is an interface that positions the relation between computer and user not as user/instrument but as a conversation between agents. When we talk to the computer, we recognize it as a companion and make sense of that companionship. Then we play.

Voice assistants are personalizations of software agencies. As interfaces, they acknowledge the agency of software, and they wrap it into a form of human, social communication. Voice assistants build on that way of relating to computers by giving them a voice and a name, by giving them personality and character, so that the implicit social relation with computers gets enhanced with the social connotations of speech and conversation. In other words, computers gain a literal voice to express the personalities we ascribe to them in our interactions.

There are of course other alternatives to these ways of creating an experiential wrapper around the social relations we establish with computers. The creative communities around artificial intelligence have been exploring playful interactions with these systems as a way to demonstrate the potential of these systems. For example, OpenAI introduced its generative text tool GPT-2 by making an interactive fiction video game *AI Dungeon*. This game overcame a frustration that many of us who grew up playing text-based adventure games know too well: the painful limits of what the text parser has been programmed to recognize. Sometimes the video game would recognize only a very simple set of sentences like "Go North" or "Look." More advanced systems recognized more combinations, but playing these games felt like being chained to a very unclever dungeon master. OpenAI's text recognition and generation are so advanced that they can recognize keywords and create coherent replies based on those keywords. In *AI Dungeon*, almost any input would be replied to with a coherent continuation of a story. *AI Dungeon 2* improved this system by limiting the possibility space available to the player: we had to choose a specific genre of interactive function in order to play. This is a system built on the pretense, upheld by the player, that the computer would understand and react to the prompt accordingly.

The importance of chatting as a relational, playful form of engaging with the alien agency of software has even reached space. In 2003, computer scientist Kevin Copple used the Yevpatoria radio telescope to broadcast to space the computer program Ella, which could be compiled to run as a chatbot that "enjoys playing Atlantic City blackjack, telling jokes, predicting fortunes, and reciting poems."[19] Would aliens engage with the chatbot? The fact that humans thought that it would be interesting to send a computer program that displayed an understanding of human language and a set of traits that made it identifiable as a personality points to the importance of this kind of make-believe in our understanding of software. Creating chatbots for actual aliens, or perhaps chatbots so actual aliens could engage with alien civilizations like ours, is a playful approach to engaging with our cosmic loneliness.

The importance of conversation and make-believe for engaging with software explains phenomena from ELIZA to *AI Dungeon* to outer space, from chatbots as costumer service to chatbots as ways of interstellar communication. Make-believe is essential to explain why playing software is shaping the culture of the information age.

Pretending and Making Pretense

Pretense is essential in the activity of play. All Western theories of play draw on make-believe to explain not only particular games but also the relation between play and ritual, the engagements between players, and the way the worlds of play are constructed. In their landmark work on media and play, Frissen et al. mention the importance of make-believe in our consumption and production of software as critical for understanding computational media.[20]

I am going to take that idea one step forward. For Huizinga, agonistic play was the ludic heart of culture. Other forms of play existed, and their importance was highlighted by Callois, who in his disagreement with Huizinga expanded the categories of play so that chance, vertigo, and pretense would also be considered for the study of play.[21] The importance of make-believe is such that Sutton-Smith identified it as one of the dominant rhetorics of play.[22] At this point in this book, I hope it is clear that I prefer to veer away from Huizingan tradition, so I'll take my chances and affirm that in the information age, it is play as make-believe that creates culture. The rhetoric of make-believe has become the dominant rhetoric of play.

If we narrow our perspective to video games, we may not be able to see this dominance that clearly. Video games, and all other games, are material practices of play that already require a form of active make-believe in order to exist. Once again, this is what Suits described as the "lusory attitude." I am aware that make-believe, as Caillois or Sutton-Smith define it, is relatively different from what Suits writes about. But the phenomenon of *pretending* that the rules of a game are binding, that winning is important, that the goals of a game are meaningful, these are all related to pretense, to make-believe. The worlds created by play require the pretense of their being real. Video games show us how playing as a way of dealing with and relating to worlds created by computers requires a form of make-believe.

Beyond video games, the importance of make-believe is more present in the way we interact with software. Reeves and Nass identified how we treat computers and media as part of a social relation. That relation is one of make-believe, pretending that these software programs have a form of agency we can recognize. Pretense has been essential in understanding the construction of the self toward others. From Goffman to Cohen, the construction of the self as a process is central to understanding human agency and how we relate to others, and to the world around us.[23] Following this line of thinking, I propose that make-believe is the form of play that has the most importance in shaping the culture of the information age. Let me give some examples to support this argument.

Facebook, Twitter, Instagram: all of these social networks depend on competitive mind tricks to keep us returning to them. From likes to retweets to shares to followers, we are fed numbers that allow us to compete with others. We can read these environments through the lens of Suitsian play, as C. Thi Nguyen does. Social networks then become the place for the agonistic play of performing our online personas. But the original pleasures and sins of these platforms can also be read not as the outcome of competitive play but as the result of make-believe: pretend that we are connected, that we are friends, that we live lives so interesting that they are shared and inspire others. Social media are designed to reinforce the idea that we can be a personality that resonates with the world.

Playing software is making sense through the pleasurable lens of the ludic of how those processes of self-presentation are possible. That making sense is driven by the pretense of software having agency. Play creates culture, and the culture of the information age derives from the importance of make-believe in our relations with software.

Make-believe's importance in shaping the culture of the information age resides explicitly in how it turns software systems like Alexa or Twitter into *playthings*. Using computers for aiding in work and automating tasks is the reason we have computers. Improving the ways we engage with those systems, from keyboard and mouse to visual and audio-driven interfaces, has been crucial in making computers ubiquitous systems. Alexa and Siri and the Google Home, but also Twitter, Facebook, Instagram, and TikTok, are the next step into the process of making these vast systems of agential software more mundane. When these systems become more mundane, we begin to treat them as social agents.

Voice assistants are software with proper names, voices, and elements of personality sufficiently detailed that users can interact with them, as if they actually were more than machines running instructions on data. Personality design and particularly those elements of the personality design that are not instrumental to achieving a particular goal, like the capacity to tell jokes, are the design cues that turn the interaction and relation with Alexa into the entanglement with a plaything.

This process of entanglement with a software plaything through make-believe is not limited to personalities. We can use this conceptual approach to understand the appeal of software-driven social media like Instagram or TikTok, designed to reward and encourage the creation and performance of personality. The agency of the software systems in these social networks is obviously different than it is in AI-driven voice assistants. These systems' agency relates to the distribution of images and content, to the rewarding of performance, to the filtering of what is seen and how it is seen.

To "succeed" in these forms of social media, it is necessary to grasp how recommendations and the distribution channels for videos and images work—the kind of subtle understanding of cybernetic systems that "influencers" have. One way of engaging with that software agency that can help distribute and popularize images is to create a role-playing character that will be picked up and distributed by that software. "Making" it on these social networks can imply creating and practicing a persona in a process of make-believe.[24] We can understand that process using play as an angle of inquiry, understanding how the quantification systems in these social networks are connected to pretense and make-believe, how they are not necessarily that dissimilar from *Dungeons and Dragons*. And by performing that change of perspective, we can argue that the playful form of make-believe is helping to shape the way the cultures of social media that distribute content are also a part of a ludic culture.

Personalities and Playthings

Make-believe is a specific playful strategy that makes playthings out of software agents, so the interactions with them become more pleasant, interesting, and fun. Personality design is a productive approach to facilitate this make-believe engagement.[25] It is also an illustration of a deeper cultural and social displacement of competition as the main form of play in relation to software. In this penultimate section of the chapter, I return to voice assistants to illustrate the potential of this analytical perspective and what we can learn from play and personalities when designing interfaces with software.

In *Anatomy of an AI System*, Kate Crawford and Vladan Joler mapped the deep geographies of an Alexa device. Seeing the flow of data and the distributed computational processes that make that system work, it seems unfathomable that just talking to that unobtrusive piece of technology is invoking a hidden network of systems, policies, and economics as vast and predatory as an empire. We users settle with asking Alexa to do something with and for us: talk to us about the weather, tell us what the time is, find and purchase something for us, entertain us. Alexa will be there, listening, monitoring us, and according to some patents filed by Amazon in the late 2010s, potentially even caring for us.[26]

Voice assistants are sold to us as restless secretaries, but also as the helpful, mother-like instantiations of a loving corporation; a surrogate for the parental figures some privileged brats left behind when they went to college; parents who would always listen and cater to their children's needs while they focused on their future career and successes.[27] In their absence, Alexa takes care of them, does the shopping, reminds them to dress appropriately for the weather, attends to all their needs and some of their desires. Alexa responds to the ideal of a mother/female role that many young Silicon Valley engineers seem to have in mind when designing technology and services: labor and commerce hides in commands and prompts, the results of the economic exchange hidden by glossy technologies so as to not think about the human and environmental abuse they often depend on. The warmth of Alexa and Siri, the way they seem to care about us, invokes a particular social relation based on a particular understanding of concern.

But that is just one social frame. Another social frame is that of Alexa, Siri, and the Google Assistant as impish characters who are always present, always helpful, and moderately playful in their way of acting. That is why these systems are designed with a sense of humor: so that our interactions with them are framed from a social perspective partially defined by play. Adding humor to the interaction possibilities of these assistants is an ineffiency. Instead of fulfilling their roles, these systems add humor to be just slightly inefficient, just too personal to be purely instrumental.

In our computationally mediated lives, Alexa and Siri are not the visible ends of a complex system of interconnected computational and economic resources: they are characters living in our world. Through make-believe, we relate to them as personalities, opening the doors to these vast networked systems. We pretend they care about us, entertain us, make our lives more productive and more efficient. Their personalities are instruments that help accept the place these computational agents have in our lives. We construct a world together with them, so they have a place in our social lives.

Giving personalities to things is a way of making them enter into a social relation with other agents. This form of animistic design is well known and is partially rooted in the importance of make-believe and socialization in our perception of the mediating role of technologies in the world.[28] Giving a personality to software, which is already an agent when it mediates the human experience of the world, is a direct avenue to explore the ways in which it can enter into a social relation. The characters "Alexa" or "Siri" are ways of facilitating a relation with the agency of software. The personality design of software illustrates how make-believe becomes a critical mode of play, as it is a lens through which it is possible to deal with the agency of software.

Personalities are an explicit example of this role of make-believe. But in our conversations, we are also talking about "the algorithm" acting. We have all seen a picture or gotten a TV show recommended because of "the algorithm." An algorithm does not have intentions. But pretending it has a personality, pretending that it can *decide and act*, is a way of explaining the effects that the algorithm has in our life. Reeves and Nass were right: we treat computers as social agents. Software societies are also make-believe societies, because make-believe is not just the act of pretending that a set of rules is important, that a software society exists, but also that our agency in that society is determined by and dependent on software. Make-believe explains the personalities given to computers and explains how we voluntarily adapt to the social roles given to software. Make-believe is a central strategy in understanding and living in the information age.

Worlds of Make-Believe

We cannot understand the world of the information age without understanding software agencies. From medicine (machine learning used to develop new drugs), to economics (algorithmic trading), education (game-based learning), and politics (social media populisms), all aspects of human knowledge, and therefore culture and social structures, have been affected by and changed by software.

Here we are, surrounded by computational agents, and craving for more. We have learned to relate to them in many different ways. Work helps us understand why computers can facilitate some tasks in particular ways, from number crunching to typing texts together with many others. Social practices help us understand how computers can keep us together even when we are apart, building and extending our remote connections. And play makes software an instrument for pleasure and control, often positive, sometimes an instrument to enslave us while we agree to play by its rules. In the case of play, the relation is established mostly through pretense and make-believe.

Software with personalities is the spearhead of this relational mode of making sense of artificial agency. But it is not the only mode of pretense play in the information age. Part of the process of relating to artificial agency consists of creating human personalities that become visible to software agents. To be in the information age is also to be in relation to software. We create personalities so we can also be agents in this world.

We role-play too. The creation of personalities in world traveling is not an exclusive of software; it is part of what all agents do when playing software. For example, the two most popular and successful massively multiplayer online role-playing games (MMORPG) of all time are Instagram and Tinder. They are windows to simpler, streamlined lives that are shown to others, distributed globally, and accessible to the observing eye of quantification systems. Our lives on Instagram are lives of pretense. Nobody's life is as interesting, ironic, or coherent as it is on Instagram. We all role-play in these settings. We all create characters, frame our actions, and act as if this is our life.

Of course, this is a presentation of the self in everyday life, as sociologist Ervin Goffman described on the eve of the information age. The quantified reward structure in social media, the capacity to collectively weave stories together by writing on each other's feeds, the acknowledgment of "good gameplay" through likes, and the way the software rewards and encourages creativity allow us to look at them from the perspective of play.

And what do we gain from that perspective? For one, we can look at Instagram as a plaything. By doing so, we can apply the knowledge we have about games to consider it a role-playing game engine, with structures and systems designed to reward one-to-many social presentation with ludic logics. Instagram is also a storytelling engine, a version of *Dungeons and Dragons* that lets us become who we want to be toward others and rewards us from doing so while data mining our identity desires.

Instagram is not a game, but it can be a plaything. In certain contexts of use, it is a plaything that can be explained as a game. We may make sense of this software's agency through the lens of the ludic, placing it in our culture. In its particular interface, there is more human agency, more instrumentality in the engagement with the agency of software. But it is still a negotiation of agency, a way of using algorithmic tools to engage with the world, to create a persona. And doing so can be explained through the lens of make-believe.

This lens of make-believe exposes a dark side of computational play: the danger of agonistic quantification of self-creation. Social media that draw on make-believe are also systems to observe integers increase, from likes and retweets to followers and replies. The inherent pleasure of make-believe lies in the performance of the self, in the creation and action on personalities. Games have capitalized on that pleasure by situating in the context of agonism, for example, in role-playing games like *Dungeons and Dragons*. But in those contexts, there is an implicit negotiation that the agonistic element of performing a personality is tied to that very performance; that is, agonism is subservient to make-believe. The fun in playing *Dungeons and Dragons* is that we know, and we have agreed on, that what we're doing is playing a game.

In social media, make-believe by design is an instrument for competition. The personality is graded and evaluated through quantification, locking make-believe in a forever-looping performance of numeric engagement. Even though the results are different, this process is similar to what Dow-Schüll described in her analysis of gambling machines: the promise of another world tightly connected to quantification of action.[29] This is a danger of computational play, one that creates an iron cage of pleasure in which the performance of the self is quantified, as part of a data-extractive economy, so users get stuck in the agonistic loop of numerical engagement without enjoying the potential pleasures of make-believe.

Artist Ben Grosser has been experimenting with demetricators as instruments to highlight the damages that quantification and agonism create through social media.[30] If we install one of Grosser's demetricators, the quantified aspect of a social network becomes hidden, and that changes our experience of that network. Twitter is not about collecting retweets, and Instagram is not about performing so we get more likes. By erasing numbers, Grosser shows us how the personalities that prevail in those social networks are those who engage with them through agonistic play. Given the damaging effects of social media in Western culture, such as the rise of the Far Right and the antivaccination communities, it is important to wonder the role of agonistic play in fostering those ideas by pandering to demagogic personalities and making them "win."

There is also hope in make-believe. Playing software is world traveling toward others that include human and artificial agents, in order to meet them and create a world together. That world need not be the one we live in. Playing software allows us to reconfigure our relations to others through software and to software itself. Playing software can be the imagination and action of all the possible different others we want to be. Make-believe allows us to image other possible worlds, and playing software allows us to live in those worlds.

Personalities, both given to software and created by humans in the interface, are ways of articulating how we engage with computational systems as playthings. Personalities open up for the possibilities of make-believe as a way of playfully structuring what we do with and to computers, how we interact with them, how we make sense of them. The main revolution in the information age has been the creation of multiple interfaces to software agencies, interfaces that change the nature of the world by the mere act of existing. The way role playing helps us understand these worlds, their rules, and how they present themselves to us is critical to understand the role of play in the information age.

We ought to understand these personalities critically. Why do we want Siri to be funny? Who does Instagram want me to be? Personality design can be used as an instrument for reducing our actions to computable data. It can also be used to better understand artificial agency. Playing software is not just a matter of make-believe; it is also about the ethos of that pretense. The dominant use of personality design in the information age has been to ease the adoption of predatory data-gathering systems, like Siri and Alexa, and to quantify behavior in make-believe for polarizing emotions, as in social media. The challenge we have ahead is to image what alternatives we can propose to personality design and how care, empathy, fun, and humor could guide a more loving engagement with the designed personalities of artificial agents.

Playing software requires make-believe to facilitate relating to artificial agents, but also to make it possible for us to imagine the different worlds we are traveling to. If we wrestle make-believe from the hands of digital capitalism, we may have a way of better understanding how we can create better worlds for all of us to inhabit. Without make-believe, without this playful world traveling to meet software agencies, what is left of the information age is machines performing processes among humans.

5

Systems

In the information age, everything seems to be a system: the economy, the workplace, the way football teams play, the hierarchies in high school, the infrastructures that bind us together, and the politics that drive us apart. In a computational world, our agency and the agency of the nonhuman agents that surround us seem to be always understood as parts of a system.

This way of thinking is a consequence of systems thinking, a discipline pioneered by Jay Forrester that studies the formal properties and the interrelations among phenomena.[1] Initially applied to business flows and studies of the processes of information transmission, systems thinking became extremely popular in the 1970s and 1980s as an epistemology that could provide novel insights in how the world works, from the economy to learning and human relationships. In her work *Thinking in Systems*, Donella Meadows carefully proposes the use of concepts from systems thinking to explain multiple phenomena in the world.[2] For Forrester and Meadows, the concept of systems is epistemological; that is, it is a concept and a methodology for describing phenomena.

However, the concept of systems is often used not as a method for describing the world but as an ontology. We have grown used to applying the concept of "systems" to define the nature of things rather than as a method for studying phenomena. I use ontology here to describe the study of what things *are*. Epistemology is the study of how we create knowledge about things. These are two very different things, and confusing them can have unforeseen consequences.

As I wrote earlier, we tend to think that the economy and politics are systems, their nature being that of processes and flows. This is a reductionist approach. If everything is a system, phenomena like affect, solidarity, empathy, or the myriad of different constellations of human togetherness become difficult to observe, relate to, or value. Systems thinking is alluring because it identifies the complexities of the world that go beyond what we can intuitively understand, but it is dangerous in that it can be used to reduce the complexity and richness of existence, both human and nonhuman, to processes of interaction and information exchange.

The concept of systems and the epistemology of systems thinking are interesting because play and systems are intrinsically related. Games are made of, among other things, systems of rules designed to structure behavior. Similarly, software is also heavily reliant on systems—processes and operations on data that are formally structured so they can be computable. The concept of systems can be used to describe both play and software.

In this chapter, I study this relation between play and systems using Norbert Wiener's cybernetics as a starting point. This chapter is fairly academic in its structure, presenting each premise of the argument as related to a body of literature that explains the argumentation. The reason for this stylistic shift is my intention to address seriously a complex and polemic topic: online-driven conspiracy theories and disinformation. There is a wealth of excellent scholarship on online disinformation, and my intention with this chapter is to provide a complementary angle to that conversation.[3]

My argument begins with the adoption of Wiener's concept of entropy to inquire about how computers create worlds that offer stability and order against the encroaching of entropy. From Wiener I shift toward video games, looking at the importance of the concept of systems in their design. I use video games because they are the most representative media of the playful information age, but these reflections about the design of playable systems should echo in other forms of playable software.

The third step in this chapter is a dangerous one: Drawing on the analysis that some game designers did of the conspiracy theory known as QAnon, I explore the temptations of system thinking, how these temptations are reinforced by computer programs, and what the dangers are of playing software. The chapter closes with a reflection on the limits of play as an analytical lens, drawing a parallel with the limits of the concept of system when it comes to addressing the complexities of lifeworlds.

Cybernetics and Entropy

Norbert Wiener's cybernetics theory provides an important angle to understand the importance of the concept of systems in the intellectual argumentations and technological developments of software. Wiener's theory is too complex to quickly summarize it in a brief chapter, so my take will be reduced to engaging with the concepts of control and entropy as presented in *The Human Use of Human Beings*.[4]

Wiener's cybernetic theory is a mathematical and philosophical framework that addresses the role of communication and control. He famously defined the discipline as the science of control and communications in the animal and the machine. At the end of World War II, it was evident to many US-based scientists that communication and the machines that mediate that communication are central to understanding the world. Cybernetics is one of the theories that came about in the paradigmatic change in the sciences and the humanities that happened in the mid-twentieth century.

Wiener's concept of cybernetics went beyond studying communication. He saw cybernetics as a philosophical framework, a way of explaining the world, especially society, that "can only be understood through a study of the messages and the communication facilities which belong to it, and that in the future development of these messages and communication facilities, messages between man and machines, between machines and man, and between machine and machine, are destined to play an ever-increasing part. . . . Communication and control belong to the essence of man's inner life, even as they belong to his life in society."[5]

For cybernetics, the relations between agents in the world can be understood as exchanges of information, that is, as communication. This communication is structured through mechanisms of control that facilitate the correct transmission and reception of information. These mechanisms of control, like feedback loops and sensors, help agents make sense of the world and other agents and to communicate in effective ways. Cybernetics' central assumption is that entropy in an informational world is inevitable and that communication and its mechanisms are attempts at controlling and even reversing entropy locally. The world tends toward disorder, but its agents strive for order through control.

Systems are, from a cybernetic perspective, the instruments that can be applied to ensure communication and stave off entropy. Wiener's central insight is that this application of mechanisms to create control and communication is analogous in humans and machines, more specifically computers: "The machine, like the living organism, is, as I have said, a device which locally and temporarily seems to resist the general tendency for the increase of entropy. By its ability to make decisions it can produce around it a local zone of organization in a world whose general tendency is to run down."[6]

The importance of control and entropy in cybernetics is central to my argument. In this view, the world's tendency to entropy can be reduced in encapsulations. In the vocabulary of this book, order can be established in temporary worlds, which are created to increase information. And these worlds are not exclusively human: "Machines also contribute to a local and temporary building up of information, notwithstanding their crude and imperfect organisation compared to that of ourselves."[7]

The era of cybernetics is characterized by local reductions of entropy though order and control effected through systems—hence, the centrality of Wiener in our understanding of systems. Systems allow for the constructions of worlds of order in which information exchange is possible. In these worlds, human and machine agents exchange information mediated by those very systems.

The development and popularity of systems theory can be traced back to this argumentation. Systems are instruments for order. They allow hybrid worlds of human and machine agencies to work together and effectively communicate. Through control, "the mechanical tendency towards disorganization is not only reduced but also reversed, and society can be studied."[8] Forrester and Meadow's work on modeling the world through systems is a direct result of Wiener's work.

Wiener saw in computers new possibilities for control and communication. What I describe in this book as software agency would be, in Wiener's cybernetics take, a consequence of the capacity of machines to use mechanisms of control to create effective communication and thus reverse entropy. Through feedback mechanisms and sensors, the interaction between software/machines and humans would allow for the creation of worlds that are orderly, created against encroaching entropy.

From a cybernetics perspective, order and control create worlds that are stable. In these worlds, communication and agency between humans and machines is possible. "Systems" are the conceptual tools, the instruments that allow the analysis of cybernetic worlds that tend toward stability and how they stabilize themselves.

The cybernetic importance of control and order should immediately resonate with play scholars. Huizinga's claim that play is essential in the creation of culture is rooted in his understanding of play's capacity to create order, specifically through rules that clearly delimit agonistic conflicts. From the rules of contests to the law to games themselves, play studies has acknowledged the importance of rules in the creation of the worlds we play in. There are of course forms of play that are destructive, that are focused on chaos and disorder, but in this chapter, my interest focuses on the intersection between games as creators of order and cybernetics as the study of control and communication, particularly with attention to software-mediated order.[9]

The observation that play and cybernetics are related is not new. Foundational works in game studies and in posthumanism already understood the importance of this relation,[10] and media studies has explored the intersection of cybernetic theory, capital, and play before.[11] I make an argument in this tradition, contributing to the broader conversation around cybernetics. Video games are an example of how, through systems of rules encoded in software, human and artificial agencies create worlds of order in which new relational forms of being can take place. The interface is a place of order, crafted by the rules of software and, in the case of video games, also by the rules of a game. Playing video games is not just *playing video games*: it's engaging in the practice of relating to the alien agencies of software in the ordered world created by rules of the game and the rules of software.[12]

All video games are a relational engagement with cybernetic order. Playing a video game to win is a struggle to consummate the purpose of that world.[13] Playing a game to not lose is a lesson in the futility of fighting entropy. Playing an infinite game, cultivating crops in *Stardew Valley* or paying off a mortgage in the *Animal Crossing* series is an act of creative stewardship on that world, helping to maintain the order the rules have given us.[14] Video games give us the comfort of order and the possibility of acting together and relating to other agents in a way that becomes meaningful and pleasurable.

Software operates in the same way. By formalizing the context and the processes that are relevant for computations, software can become an agent toward which we can relate. For example, the transformation of the human step into a collection of data points to be read by sensors and processed by an algorithm creates a world where those steps exist. Similarly, if certain skin colors are not part of the data used to formalize procedures, the processes enacted by that software will not allow everybody to become part of that world.[15]

The rules of software can be opaque; they are often part of a complex technical process that has been mystified and made distant by those who write software, who would rather make the world magical than comprehensible.[16] Playing software is establishing relations with the alien agency of software. That process is cybernetic; it implies engaging with systems that create a world that is ordered. In that world, agency is delimited and framed by clear rules voluntarily accepted. The purpose and the meaning of the activities in that world are a consequence of relating to those rules either constructively or destructively. Play creates order; playing software creates cybernetic order.

This argument was quickly adopted by game scholars with an interest in the formal study of games and game design, leading to an adoption of the concept of systems as central for game design. Let's look closer at the adoption of this cybernetic argument in game design theory.

Systems and Game Design

Game design literature has been aware of the importance of cybernetic concepts almost from its inception. Sudnow's phenomenological-inspired reflections on his experiences with games were hinting at the importance of systems in the creation of the perceptual and experiential gestalts of video game play.[17] In Salen and Zimmerman's classic *Rules of Play*, chapter 18 is dedicated to the study of games as cybernetic systems, providing a valuable primer for game designers in the importance of cybernetic concepts.[18] The use of the concept of systems is critical in game design research, and it has been used to argue for the potential of video games as a cultural and educational platform.[19]

Game designers create playable experiences, crafting worlds through rules that set the stage for relational engagements between players and nonhuman agents. By studying the way systems are formalized for game designers, relating them to classic systems theory studies, I study an ideology of systems in the design of playable software. While my reflection will be limited to video game design, the arguments here should be easy to observe in other forms of playable media presented throughout this book.

This section focuses on one game design text, Zubek's *Elements of Game Design*,[20] not only because it is an excellent textbook but also because of the importance of the author's work in a certain systems-aware way of teaching and reflecting on game design.[21] I briefly engage with Zubek's application of systems thinking to establish the roots of this particular approach to game design in systems thinking. I apply Zubek's work to present how video game design can be a cybernetic practice.

Zubek's excellent pedagogics of game design never forgets that the design of any playable media is the design of a mediated experience. Zubek makes it very clear that his goal is to formalize for educational purposes how games are constructed, so that game design can become a teachable practice. Looking at the pedagogics of game design makes sense for the purpose of my argument, as good design teaching is based on explaining the principles behind materials and the practices of a particular field.

In this sense, Zubek's application of the concept of systems illustrates well how video games are understood as *designed systems*. If game educations present game design as the design of experiences through systems, then it will be fair to say that the cultural understanding of games will be mostly systems-centric. And since video games are dominant playable media of the information age, then they provide a good way to start understanding the intersection between play and software from a systems perspective.

Zubek's pedagogics are explicit about the importance of systems: "We will focus on games as systems that the player engages with, games as *machines for playing with*. Here 'machine' is a shorthand for a dynamic model, an artificial system of rules and interactions that players operate."[22] Zubek does not rule out board games or other nondigital playable media, but the idea of *machines for playing* resonates particularly well with video games. What are video games, if not machines that mediate the practice of playing software?

Therefore, the idea that video games can be understood as systems makes sense. Zubek presents his reflections on systems as an epistemological tool, as a lens to make sense of how games are constructed: "Systems are a very useful abstraction. When we try to come up with the design for a new game, we can start from mechanics. However, sometimes it is more fruitful to start the conversation on the level of entire game systems instead because that lets us paint with a larger brush . . . to start at a higher level before we come back to fill in the details."[23] A system is a way of making sense of the multiple structures of order that video games present, from rules to mechanics, understood as the actions afforded to the player in the game. Understanding video games as systems is also important since "some designers like Sellers . . . suggest that systems are *the most important* abstraction level for games because systems-based interaction is what makes games unique compared to other types of entertainment."[24]

While this intuition about the uniqueness of games can be questioned, it is important to take into consideration that video games are often understood, by audiences and designers, as collections of interactive systems that create experiences.[25] In fact, Zubek explicitly claims that "this is also our task as game designers . . . : how do we create these experiences, these worlds for the player to inhabit and interact with?"[26] Game design is the creation of worlds, structured through systems, in which human experiences happen.

Video games are software that creates worlds of order in which human experience is carefully planned and created. Any video game can be understood as a system that creates playable order. Meadows defined systems as "a set of things . . . interconnected in such a way that they produce their own pattern of behavior over time."[27] This pattern of behavior in the case of video games is not just that of the system, but of the entanglement of human and artificial agency in the world of the video game. That behavior is *playing*.

The notion of interconnections, "the relationships that hold the elements together," is at the heart of systems thinking."[28] Video games are important not because they are interactive but because they are machines that use systems to interconnect through the relationality of play, human and artificial agents.

Video games are examples of worlds created with software for human and artificial agencies to relate. The worlds created by video games are worlds of order in which designers strive for creating purpose through the affordance of action and feedback loops. This purpose creates a pleasurable experience. In this sense, video games are cybernetic systems: they create temporary pockets of order in the world in which human agency is given purpose and meaning. As game studies and design scholars have already pointed out, games are cybernetic practices.[29]

The argument could stop here. I could claim that video games are important because they show how playing software is inhabiting worlds created in the interface of human and artificial agency, how those are worlds of temporary order in an entropic universe, and how playing software creates worlds of ludic order for human and artificial agencies.

The problem is that systems thinking can also illustrate some of the perils of playing software. In fact, systems thinking understood not as a lens to understand and create the world, but as an instrument that defines the nature of things, an ontology instead of an epistemology, can be part of the problems of playing software. The worlds created by software and play can be worlds of creativity and expression, of pleasure and aesthetics, but they can also be other worlds that alienate us, separate us from others, and make us puppets of mischievous human and artificial agents. The worlds created by playing software can also be closed worlds.

Closed Worlds and the Dangers of Playing Software

The history of computing is inextricably linked to the military use of computers. Wiener's work, as well as that of Turing, Hopper, von Neumann, and many other founding parents of computation, was boosted by military investment and war efforts. The applications of computing machines to military purposes were obvious, and they still drive many of the frontlines in computer science research, from AI used for face recognition and target acquisition to cyberwarfare. But I am not interested in tracing the mostly North American imperialist drive underlying many software products. Behind the military mindset, behind the attempt at systematizing and formalizing the world so (semiautonomous) weapons can be deployed for imperialist purposes, there is a worldview. That worldview demonstrates the dangers of playing software and the pleasures and temptations of closed worlds.

In *The Closed World*, his comprehensive history of computation and the Cold War, Paul Edwards describes the logic of closed worlds as a worldview that animated the Cold War conflict, a worldview that created but was also strengthened by computers.[30] According to Edwards,

> "Closed-world discourse" thus names a language, a worldview, and a set of practices characterized in a general way by the following features and elements:
>
> - techniques drawn from engineering and mathematics for modeling aspects of the world as closed systems.
> - technologies, especially the computer, that make systems analysis and central control practical on a very large scale.
> - practices of mathematical and computer simulation of systems . . .
> - experiences of grand-scale politics as rule-governed and manipulable for example by means of the power of nuclear weapons . . .
> - fictions, fantasies, and ideologies, including such visions as global mastery through air power and nuclear weapons . . .
> - a language of systems, gaming, and abstract communication and information that relied on formalisms to the detriment of experiential and situated knowledge.[31]

The closed-world discourse describes the logics of a world understood from the perspective of systems that model reality. These systems are programmed into computer networks that enact the processes of control and communication necessary to uphold the existence of that closed world. The closed-world discourse, rooted in Cold War politics and American imperialism, is a politics of cybernetics. If Wiener's *The Human Use of Human Beings* proposed, among other things, an ethics for the era of control and communication, the closed-world discourse is a politics of systems thinking.

According to Edwards, it is possible to trace some of the political, ideological, and social discourse of the Cold War to a discourse in which systems, and the way they are analyzed through software, determine a particular imperial logic. In the closed world, the imperialist dream of control and communication of the world through engineering is facilitated by the logics of systems implemented in software.

The closed world has its own logic, one in which the human, the "experiential and situated knowledge," is downplayed in favor of the logic of systems that allow for control. The closed world promises control, facilitated through communication systems, and that control will ensure that empires will prevail. It is a closed world in which formal categories can be deployed to manage through rules the population of the world.

The closed-world discourse echoes what Dyer-Witheford and De Peuter wrote in *Games of Empire*: how (video)games can be used as instruments for promoting an ideology of imperialism that normalizes the expansion of superpowers.[32] Video games can also act as instruments of the closed-world discourse, especially propagandistic video games that allow players to enact imperialistic dreams of global control.

The closed-world discourse is partially based on cybernetics and its interest in control and communication in a world of information formalized as systems. From military exercise games to role-playing games to video games, playable media were used as an instrument to teach and indoctrinate in the language of the closed world. The military use of computer games and the military discourse in computer games both draw on the pleasures of play to streamline the ideology of the closed world.

There is a more dangerous element in the closed-world discourse: it can become a form of comfort. Order and control through systems and the devices that support those systems fulfill the promise of cybernetics: pockets of order in a world of entropy. The closed world gives order to the world. Within its closed environment, within its logic, there is order. In that closed world, the instruments and tools for control and communication satisfy those who live in that world. It can be reassuring, in the face of chaos, to stay within the closed world.

This pleasure of being in the closed world is analogous to the pleasure of being in a game, engaged and captivated by a world of order. Computational systems can reinforce the structure of this closed world, enhancing our control over that environment and our capacity to have agency. These systems can be designed and presented to us as order in a world of chaos. Cybernetic systems thinking can lead to closed-world discourses, in which the logic of computation is extended beyond machines. Machine agency becomes the model to follow, and human agency becomes reduced to what can be computed.

This is a critical aspect of the closed world and a certain logic of cybernetics. In the closed world, what counts as existing is what can be calculated by software. The artist Kyle McDonald is behind the website plaything *Facework*, a short game-like experience that illustrates how computers see the world. In the narrative of the game, the player is a worker in the gig economy that needs to audition for different jobs. Each job has some requirements, like wearing a mask, smiling, or frowning. Players use their webcams to respond to the games' requests. By doing so, players are exposed to what machine vision systems can see and how a "smile" is not necessarily a smile but what can be computed as a smile (figure 5.1). Playing *Facework* is exploring the rift between the messy and ambiguous human world, and the strict and orderly world of software, in which to be is to be computed.

This modulation of agency to become part of a world of order is something that we are already aware of: that is how play has created culture since the beginning of times. Play promises order and meaning within a closed world as long as rules are followed. It is not binding us to blindly follow rules; it is promising agency within the limits of a closed world. These are the implications of Salen and Zimmerman's famous description of play as free movement in a bound environment.

Game designers use the language of systems and cybernetics because making games creates pleasurable closed worlds, pockets of order that have meaning and give purpose to actions. When software is played, the pleasures of those ludic closed worlds, of those coherent pockets of order we inhabit because we want to have fun, become part of the experience. Playing software makes the technologies that are the foundation for closed-world discourses more pleasurable.

Figure 5.1
Kyle McDonald's *Facework*. Author's screenshot.

When systems are created as instruments to create order, play becomes a relational mode of entangling with those systems. If the systems that drive the recommendation engines in social media favor particular behaviors, we will pivot to acting in those ways because that is the playable logic of that closed world. Instagram can become a role-playing engine, as can Twitter: those are worlds in which there is order through make-believe, supported and encouraged by actions that quantify the quality of that behavior. The gamified interfaces of social media are reinforcing a particular logic of communication as a game that can be quantified and won. The internal logics of Instagram or Twitter and closed-world discourses reinforces patterns of behavior (presentation of the self, communication) and rewards them with being seen by the software, being promoted by it. Complying with the rules of social media means becoming visible within that closed world.

All forms of play create order, from the quantified order of competition to the performative order of pretense. In this sense, the magic circle of play can be understood as a cybernetic closed world in which particular forms of agency are encouraged.

Software and play promise order in chaos, and both are related through the notion of systems: systems can order the world through software; play can make those systems pleasurable: systems can reinforce the behavioral loops that create pleasure, shaping human agency. Closed worlds can be accessed through software, through play, or through both. These closed worlds provide the thrills of play with the systemic reinforcement behavioral loops of software.

The promise of order in the confusion of life makes both software and play highly attractive propositions. The presence of software in all elements of our lives, and the way it has helped structure mass communication through the internet, has also created new variations of closed-world discourses. Paraphrasing Edwards, the fantasies of imperialist power, the importance of games of logic and puzzles, and the understanding of politics as rule-based systems are all a fundamental part of mass communication through social media mediated by computers.

Since play is a relational form of making sense of software and also a form of creating closed-world discourses through systems, it is not surprising that communication through software also leads to play-driven modes of being in the world. That is, it is not surprising that phenomena from the online world can be understood as acting like a form of play, most typically like a game.

A Most Dangerous . . . Game?

In September 2020, Reed Berkowitz published an analysis of the QAnon conspiracy theory from a game designer's perspective.[33] Based on his experience with alternate reality games, Berkowitz described the main characteristics of the QAnon phenomenon from the perspective of the entanglement of human psychology and systems development that is game design. Before I continue, it is important to state that QAnon and other conspiracy theories that threaten the well-being of Western democracies are not games. I am arguing here for the application of a ludic lens to explain how these phenomena can be traced back to a cybernetic view of the world in the context of closed-world discourses. This perspective can become useful in identifying and creating tactics to destabilize these closed worlds

QAnon is a conspiracy theory that emerged from the corners of the internet as a synthesis of different conspiracies that were brewing on anonymous internet forums like 4chan and 8chan since the mid-'00s.[34] I am not interested in the narrative details of this conspiracy, but in the way it was read as a game experience. According to Berkowitz, QAnon was "a game that plays people." The fact that QAnon is structured around unfinished and vague clues that are left for a community to put together makes it seem like an alternate reality game or a live-action, role-playing game since "it uses many of the same gaming mechanisms and rewards. It has a game-like feel," according to Berkowitz.

That game-like feel is what interests me. Again, QAnon is not a game; in fact, if anything, it is a corruption of the game logic that provides meaning to players who voluntarily abide by the rules. As Berkowitz puts it, "there is no reality here, no actual solution in the real world. Instead, this is a breadcrumb trail AWAY [sic] from reality." But it operates much like a game. It is based on "the thrill of discovery, the excitement of the rabbit hole, the acceptance of a community that loves and respects you. Because you were convinced to `connect the dots yourself' you can see the absolute logic of it." QAnon participants are led into a community and a world that is internally consistent, that is, ordered through rules of interpretation and of conduct and behavioral instruments similar to game mechanics and game rules.

In fact, as Berkowitz points out, "On the posting boards of QAnon . . . are lists of memes and instructions for how and where to post them as well as invitations to create and collect them. There are lists of technical resources about how to track individuals through their social media footprint, hack information to reveal the poster's locations, and use a wide assortment of tools designed to gather 'information,'" QAnon boards have game-like instructions and mechanics that form systems that can be interpreted from a ludic perspective. It is not a game, definitely not for QAnon believers, but the pleasures and the logics of its structure are definitely game-like.

That likeness of QAnon to a game can be interpreted from the perspective of closed-world discourses based on systems thinking derived from cybernetics. For the participants in these conspiracy theories, internet communities seem to have become pockets of control and order in an otherwise chaotic world. In that online world, a community of fellow thinkers can meet and use specific tools (mechanics) to address puzzles they can solve through their effort, a process that is individually and collectively rewarding as it is acknowledged by the community of that closed world.[35]

Being in the closed world of QAnon can be pleasurable, exhilarating, empowering. Experientially, these closed worlds can have the same thrill as playing games. But it is so only because it is a reduced world supported and facilitated by computer systems that also reward specific behaviors and actions through recommendation algorithms. These conspiracies thrive online because many corners of the internet, from Instagram to Reddit, use game-like rules and processes to create logics of closed worlds, rewarding particular behaviors with visibility and importance in those worlds. These corners of the internet, these bubbles in which conspiracies spread, are coherent worlds created by encouraging a particular, conspiratory form of agency deeply entangled with software-driven gamified reward mechanisms.[36] That closed world is the place in which a community (of play, but not just of play), meets to "solve" the world.

QAnon feels like a game because cybernetic closed worlds are closely related to games. They also show us the limits of play. QAnon and other online conspiracies that emerge in the rise of new fascisms in the Western world may seem like games, might be experienced as play, but they have none of the pleasures of play. They are interactions with systems in cybernetic loops, but they create closed worlds. Their danger comes from the proximity of these worlds to playable worlds—how they can also create cultures through order, how they can be used to propose discourses that bleed into the outside world and have an effect. These cybernetic closed worlds, facilitated by software that enhances the effects of feedback loops through recommendation patterns and data mining, are the results of interacting with systems created to foster closed-world discourses.

In order to make the QAnon conspiracy a success, its community uses approaches to media consumption that are analog to playing video games. In doing so, QAnon creates an alternative world in which those systems, those rules, create a world with internal consistency in which truth is subordinate to the rules and processes of that community and the software used to stay in touch. Whomever makes the best interpretation of the latest "drop" climbs to the algorithmic top of the attention mountain. From a cybernetic perspective, systems create worlds, and situate agents, human and artificial, in those worlds, modulating their agency. QAnon, like games, uses systems to create a closed world, and that is why it can be studied from the perspective of play, even if it is not play.

Is this, however, the destiny of play in the information age: to create closed worlds that reinforce the ideas inside those worlds, that create a form of banality of evil that justifies any action as long as it is systemically possible within the new worlds created?[37] It is certainly one of the most important contributions of play to the culture of the information age, the creation of worlds for conspiracists, harassers, and the scum of the earth to create and live in and promote worlds and cultures of exclusion, of racism, of hate.

These closed worlds are not reduced to online hate. At the time of writing this chapter, the tech world was taken over by hype surrounding blockchain-based nonfungible tokens (NFTs). Essentially, these NFTs are unique digital artifacts based on a verifiable and immutable entrance in a blockchain. NFTs were marginally popular until they were presented through the lens of play in games that allowed players to play to earn tokens that have an economic value. Playing became coupled with the extractivist logics of exploitative blockchain economies, trapping players in the seductive logic of using play to earn tokens of apparent economic value outside the game. This was a perversion of play as part of a computational logic of profit through financialization of the world that was marketed as a form of pleasure for everybody but profit for the few.

NFTs, crypto, the finalization of the world, or even the idea that all problems can be objectively addressed through computer programming are an ideology: the ideology of closed worlds, in which machines control formally defined inputs and outputs and "objectively" take control. Play can be used to facilitate the adoption and submission to computational forms of control, providing a pleasurable layer to perverse reductions of human agency. But there are other words in the information age, also a part of play's balancing act between order and chaos.

World Traveling in the Information Age

This chapter has approached some troublesome phenomena of the information age from the perspectives of play and cybernetics. My starting point was Wiener's original cybernetic theory and how his argument that through the application of the concepts of systems and communication, it was possible to create worlds of order in an otherwise entropic universe. The importance of systems in game design, and how this field appropriated systems thinking, served as a bridge to present the central argument of the chapter: both play and software can be studied and understood as systems that create worlds of order and that it is precisely that order that makes playing software pleasurable and fulfilling.

However, playing software is not always liberating. Using Edwards's concept of closed-worlds discourses, I argued that phenomena like the conspiracy theory of QAnon can be studied as a play phenomenon that creates a closed world of exclusion and hatred. Through the systemic structure of a conspiracy theory and using methodologies of game design (of playing software), the QAnon conspiracy parasitizes the pleasures of play to create chaos.

I will finish this chapter on a tone of hope. The pull of play in the information age as an interface to computational systems might be leading us to a world of online conspiracies, gamified warehouses, and playable quantified selves—a world that would be closing in on ourselves and not allowing us to see others, or really any other alternative to living in that world. But a playful approach to software can help us move away from these closed worlds.

I don't want to draw this hope exclusively on the Romantic idea of play being a human expression, because it is not enough. Play in the information age is about the human and the nonhuman, about multiple agencies and their togetherness. I want to sketch a different genealogy of hope for play.

Let's start by becoming skeptical of games—not necessarily of games per se, but of the way we use them to think about systems, worlds, and play when we think about software, from video games to gamification. In *The Utopia of Rules*, David Graeber writes, "Games allow us our only real experience of a situation where all this ambiguity is swept away. Everyone knows exactly what the rules are. And not only that, people actually *do* follow them. And by following them, it is even possible to win! This . . . is the source of the pleasure. Games, then, are a kind of utopia of rules."[38] Graeber juxtaposes the pleasure of following rules to a reflection on play as a more generative, free, potentially chaotic, and also potentially fruitful take on play. He argues that bureaucracies are afraid of that form of play and hints at the potential of play to come up with alternatives to these forms of order, an argument that echoes some of the anarchists' theories of play.[39]

Video games will not provide us with the right approach to propose how to use play to relate to software systems in an emancipatory way. This is not to say that it is not possible to use video games as frameworks for that liberation, but they tend to create closed world discourses. We need to think about systems and play differently. Wiener's work provided an initial foundation for a cybernetics that was aware of human value and values: "In a very real sense we are shipwrecked passengers on a doomed planet. Yet even in a shipwreck, human decencies and human values do not necessarily vanish, and we must make the most of them. We shall go down, but let it be in a manner to which we may look forward as worthy of our dignity."[40]

The challenge, of course, is to specify that "manner." Let's return to the risk of playing software: the creation of closed worlds. Closed-world discourses favor ideologies of conquer and submission, of formalisms that, as Edwards put it, succeed in "detriment of experiential and situated knowledge."[41] Closed worlds simplify our being human, our values and empathy and relational capacities and transform being into transactional exchanges with other agents. It is a logic of conquer and domination, of the individual who follows the rules and draws pleasure from the systems themselves.

This form of play relates well to classic Huizingan play, to the pleasures of worlds in which well-structured agonistic contests resolve social situations and thus create culture. We need a different form of play, to break away from closed worlds. Edwards draws on cybernetic theory and Donna Haraway to suggest alternatives to closed-world discourses. I shall draw again on María Lugones's theory of play as a way of breaking from the tyranny of a closed world cybernetic playing of systems.

Lugones's theory of play draws on a critical take on the closed-world discourse of Huizinga's theory of play, arguing that "play and playfulness have, ultimately, to do with contest, with winning, losing, battling [. . .] there are rules that inspire hostility [. . .] the agonistic traveler is a conqueror, an imperialist,"[42] The closed worlds of playing software, the online conspiracies and the propaganda video games, they are instruments that entice us with the pleasure of acknowledged and rewarded order, with purpose and meaning though conquering and mastery. Those worlds live for us, with us, and we can be in them without acknowledging others. QAnon excludes others; it's a closed world that keeps "otherness" away. Propaganda video games simplify the world into conflicts in which the first person has all the tools at hand to maintain the status quo. In the closed words of agonistic systems, we play to become instruments of empire. It is not possible to travel from closed worlds, and closed worlds are closed to those who do not want to live by those rules.

But play is not just about becoming a part of a world. In this book, I argue that play is a way of establishing relations with software and with others. These relations don't need to be relations of conquer. Lugones argues that play is "world traveling," an instrument to relate to and empathize with others, to see the world through other eyes, to understand ourselves and others, and to create *and live in* new worlds where alternative orders are possible. As Lugones puts it, "There are worlds that we can travel to lovingly and travelling to them is part of loving at least some of their inhabitants. The reason why I think that travelling to someone's 'world' is a way of identifying with them is because by travelling to their 'world' we can understand what it is to be them and what it is to be ourselves in their eyes."[43]Relational play is about that form of understanding, and playing software, engaging with these systems, should be world traveling to better understand others and ourselves in the information age.

The playable worlds of systems will try to lock us down in closed worlds of agonistic competition. This leads to the limited pleasures of play but also to a reducing of the self to the patterns commanded by systems in that closed world: "Agonistic travelers fail consistently in their attempt to travel because what they do is to try to conquer the other 'world.'"[44] Playing to win, engaging with the world to impose our order on others, forcing them to be who they need to be so that our closed world makes sense: that is the negative outcome of playing software if we think about systems as the source of pleasure and meaning.

Software and play create worlds for us to live in through our relational engagement with others. Systems structure that engagement, but they should act as the starting points for world traveling. Playing software can be a way of world traveling, a way of breaking away and breaking apart the closed worlds of agonistic imperialistic systems. We may want to play with software worlds "to take a hold of oneself and of one's relation to others in a particular 'world.' . . . One may then see what the possibilities for play are for the being one is in that 'world.' One may even decide to inhabit that self fully in order to understand it better and find its creative possibilities. All of this is just self-reflection and it is quite different from resigning or abandoning oneself to the particular construction of oneself that one is attempting to take a hold of."[45]

In the early days of the internet, the promise of becoming who we wanted to be in the network fueled a role-playing-infused utopian dream of the Web. This dream was co-opted by capital and imperialism that turned the tools of expression into tools for closed-world creation. Maybe we should think differently about the promise of a world of software. Maybe the promise is not to be who we want to be, but to be able to travel toward others, human and animal and machine, and understand them. Maybe the promise of the cybernetic world is not about the expression of the individual in freedom but about playfully being many, about understanding not what *is* for *me* but what *could be* for *us*.

Donella Meadows understood the ethical imperative in Wiener's cybernetics. For her, "Living successfully in a world of systems requires of us more than our ability to calculate. It requires our full humanity—our rationality, our ability to sort out truth from falsehood, our intuition, our compassion, our vision, and our morality."[46] Play can be an instrument to close the world, to exclude others, to impose our systems of white Western control on every *other*. But play can be, and ultimately should be, a liberating way of world traveling. Playing software should be a passport to understand others and ourselves, to propose different worlds and live in them, and do so together.

6
Capital

Pippin Barr's dystopian-realist video game, *It Is As If You Were Doing Work,* makes us play the mundanities of work in the digital age. Through its appropriation of the look of the Windows 95 and 98 interfaces. and its nihilistic take on work tasks, *It Is As If You Were Doing Work* reveals both the absurdity of (most) work and the conventions of digital systems that are supposed to facilitate productivity (figure 6.1).

In addition to its humorous take on the aesthetics of software for work, Barr's game also showcases how much of "work" has become "playable" because it is mediated through software. There is a common literacy and aesthetic in software that crosses from forms of play to forms of work: loading screens, points, rewarding sounds, and even physics engines applied to visual elements. These are all tropes that are at place in both video games and work systems. A game like Barr's is possible because many work visual interfaces are surprisingly similar to video game visual interfaces. I hope there is somewhere an evil twin of Barr's game, *It Is As If You Were Doing Play,* that dulls out the pleasures of play because it focuses exclusively on the visual imaginaries of video games.

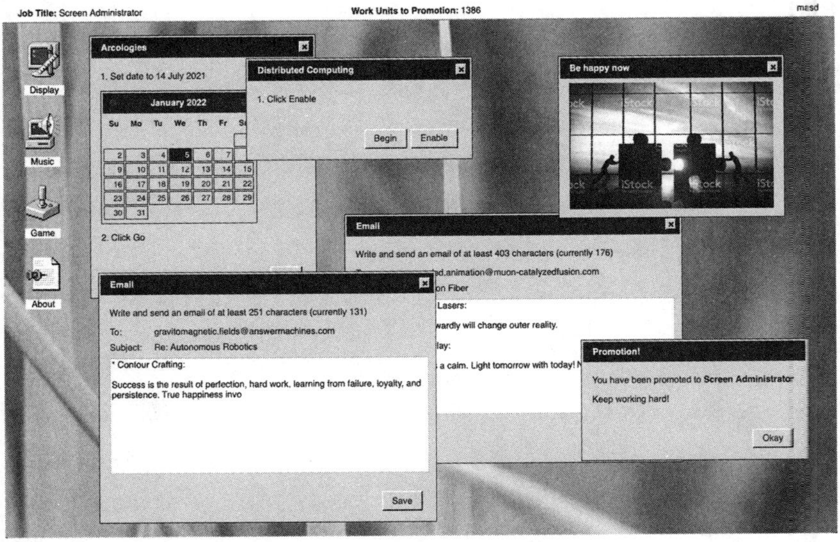

Figure 6.1
Working on Pippin Barr's *It Is As If You Were Doing Work*. Author's screenshot.

In fact, I don't need to imagine it. It already exists, and it is made by Amazon. At the beginning of the 2020s, Amazon started rolling out a gamification system in its warehouses. At that time, the exploitative working conditions in those locations had opened up Amazon for public scrutiny, revealing the software-driven dehumanization of workers. It is not clear whether Amazon developed its gamification systems as a response to labor critiques or as a natural follow-up to its software-driven quantification of workers' processes. In any case, the result was a series of "games" that were supposed to enhance workers' quality of life and help them be productive. What it ended up being was a form of play at the service of digital capitalism.

In this chapter, I situate digital play in the context of the mutant forms of capitalism that have emerged from the widespread application of software in society. In the information age, software has helped identify more resources that can be extracted from the many for the benefit of the few. For example, personal data have become a commodity that can be harvested and commercialized, with the advantage of being able to do that anywhere and typically with our consent, in exchange for software goods and services. In itself, software is not necessarily capitalist. The software I have looked at in this book is, however, the output of capitalist societies.[1] It is therefore necessary to study how it has accelerated the evolution and propagation of new modalities of capitalism, from platform capitalism to surveillance capitalism.[2] Playing software has been a critical part of this evolution, turning play into an instrument for capitalism.

Video games, the technology of play characteristic of the information age, are good examples of this appropriation of play by capitalism. These games are novel instruments for and manifestations of capitalism, pleasurable forms of ideology that propagate capitalist and imperialist ideas.[3] Even the economics of video game production are insightful examples of digital capitalism and its new ways of structuring labor and creating value.[4]

The purpose of this chapter is to provide an understanding of play as an instrument of capital. It is often easy to praise the powers of play as a liberating force, inasmuch as we don't observe playing as related to the economic forces in which it happens.[5] By contextualizing playing software in contemporary capitalism, I question what we mean by the pleasure of play when the activity of playing is part of an predatory, colonialist economic system. I want to be optimistic about play and its powers, but it is difficult to be so as digital capitalism is appropriating the discourse around the positive aspects of play to help promote new forms of exploitation.

I am not a political economist, and this is not a book about the sociology of labor. Therefore, my argument builds on theories of capitalism that draw parallels with my understanding of play. The first step is appropriating Mark Fisher's concept of capitalist realism.[6] In his analysis, capitalism thrives because it excels at promoting itself as the only possible mode of organizing the world. From politics to economics to personal relations, nothing can escape capitalism. In a capitalist realist world, corporations are using play to convince us that there is no alternative to capitalism and that capitalism itself can be pleasurable. The worlds created when playing become corrupted. This form of playing software is a form of entanglement not just with software agents but also with capitalist platforms that profit from that entanglement.

Variations on playful labor, from Amazon's gamification to free-to-play games, are used as a way of emotionally engaging users with platforms to exploit them.[7] To illustrate this role of playing software, I return to *Quick, Draw!*, the AI-powered game-like product that I introduced in chapter 3. *Quick, Draw!* is a plaything that wraps data-extractive practices under the pleasurable cover of fun and games. Digital capitalism is appropriating play as another form of labor exploitation that benefits the few and extracts from everything whatever can be commodified.

I don't want to end in despair. Lugones's understanding of play encourages the opposite of what capitalism promotes. Play is a way of finding others, of living in worlds that are possible and can be created together. The fact that digital play has been commodified does not mean that all digital play is an instrument of capital. Playing requires fun, silliness, humor, distance from rules; playing can be an act of understanding others where they are or where they are met. As Haraway has noted, "Through playful engagement with each other, we get a hint of what can still be and learn how to make it stronger."[8] Drawing again on Lugones, I finish the chapter with a sketch of a future in which play can become an emancipatory practice in digital capitalism.

Captured at Play

Software has made many types of work easier to carry out. At the same time, work has become closer to software in that repetitive tasks are now a part of both white- and blue-collar tasks. Even as an academic, much of my time is used in performing the same repetitive tasks in obscure time management interfaces. A lot of my work actually resembles Pippin Barr's game, without the pleasure of playful humor.

Gamification is an attempt of making work tasks more interesting using game design methods. Corporations like Microsoft have invested in heavily gamified services like LinkedIn, which has used competitive gameplay design to make networking feel more like a game. Gamification can also be used to play a nasty trick. Playing is a way of creating new worlds and new forms of agency, driven by pleasure and fun. The distorted logic of gamification wants to use play's mode of being in the word to become entangled with work practices and agencies. That is, we become entangled with the world of work, understood as a form of value extraction. The purpose of gamification is to create a form of agency that believes that work is fun, that it is a voluntary activity, that it is pleasurable. Yet gamification can be nothing but a form of agency manipulation disguised as (corrupted) play.

Gamification software can be used to make productivity increase while promising workers more "fun" types of engagement with work. Networking on LinkedIn can be seen as a competitive, agonistic game in which every contact is a point in a forever growing competition. Sports applications gamify health not because they care about their users, but because this is an efficient way of gathering data that can be packaged and resold, making the user a playful product.[9] The value of fun, the liberating and educational possibilities of play, is co-opted in narrow forms of competitive play that reward quantifiable and commodifiable actions.[10]

This use of play by capitalism draws on the corruption of play as a form of agency.[11] Labor exploitation adopts the capacity of play to engage pleasurably with the world to further the agenda and practices of capitalism. In this context, playing is understood as a voluntary, competitive performance. As Henricks puts it, "In play people are oriented towards satisfaction arising from their performance in the event. They desire experiences of completion, which serve as the behavior's principal rationale. And they pursue those satisfactions by actively manipulating the circumstances before them."[12] Play is also a form of agency related to order—more specifically, to the imposition, acceptance, and relation to order in the world.[13] Games provide this order explicitly thorough rules. Playable media do so by encouraging certain behaviors and rewarding them.[14] In capitalism, play is an instrument applied to create a pleasurable relation to rules while easing extractive processes. Labor and commodification become parts of play, and new forms of value extraction emerge.

A parallel phenomenon happens with propaganda games. First-person shooter games in the *Call of Honor* or *Medal of Duty* genre act as propaganda vehicles for the US Army and its presence in the world as an imperialist force. It seems that all global enemies of the United States have deserved a role in a shooter game, from Middle Eastern factions to Venezuela or even the Nazis, again and always.

The literature on these propaganda shooters is also abundant, so my contribution here will be small: these shooters are insidious because they use the capacity of play to create worlds to push players to ways of understanding the world that align with imperialist ideologies.[15] Because play creates agencies, these games quite literally create imperialist agents. If video games can be the propaganda instruments of empire, the appropriation of play by capitalism makes all forms of playable media instruments for value and labor extraction camouflaged as playful pleasurable experiences.

What happens when we interact with these types of playthings, like gamified systems and propaganda video games? Philosopher of games C. Thi Nguyen argues that often these are examples of a process that he calls value capture, a phenomenon that happens when:

1. Our values are, at first, rich and subtle.
2. We encounter simplified (often quantified) versions of those values.
3. Those simplified versions take the place of our richer values in our reasoning and motivation.
4. Our lives get worse.[16]

Gamification can make those who engage with it act on simplified versions of values, which are not only often quantified, as Nguyen argues, but also potentially encouraging the values and ideas of form of predatory capitalism.[17] When health becomes quantified, when values become statistics, and it is possible to compete on friendships or the attention we pay to each other, the user becomes the product, and the data produced in that value capture process become commodities. Nguyen argues that gamification can be a form of value capture. When gamification creates agents for work, it is value capture corrupting the activity of play.

The same happens in the case of propaganda video games. These games are designed to capture our values, simplify them, and give us a version of these values that can be used to promote imperialistic and colonialist ideas. This is not a deterministic process: many players find it possible to distance themselves from propaganda, so they can play these games without their values being substituted. And of course some gamers consume these products as a way of affirming their values and worldviews. What matters is that the nature of those video games is still propaganda, and they will succeed in capturing the values of a significant number of players.

But I don't want to talk about video games here because the role of playing as an instrument of capitalism goes beyond them. Beyond propaganda and labor exploitation in the video game industry, there are more forms of predatory capitalism making use of the agency of play. Capitalists and their ideologues can use play to promote the engagement with exploitative forms of technology. In doing so, a new mutant form of capitalism emerges: playful capitalism.

Playful Capitalism

To understand play in the context of digital capitalism, I need to retell the central argument of this book: for software to have agency in the world, it requires its precise rules and processes to be followed and related to by all other agents around it. One way of accepting rules as a form of order in the word is through play. If software becomes a plaything, its rules are easier to accept as part of the pleasurable entanglement of agencies that happens when playing. Playful capitalism appropriates that entanglement to profit from pleasurable engagement.

Play is making sense of and acting within rules. It also suggests that the rules that bind agents are accepted voluntarily and that they are true in the moment. Play makes rules valid in a particular point in time but does not care about the meaning and impact of the rules beyond the activity. The rules of a game are relevant only while playing the game. When digital forms of capitalism turn interactions with software into forms of play, they do so to prevent critical engagement with the infrastructures and apparatuses of oppression.[18]

Which form of capitalism benefits from the cooptation of play as an instrument? So far I have waved my arms and mentioned capitalism, digital capitalism, and platform capitalism as vague notions that are supposed to point in the direction of all manifestations of capitalism that are inextricable from the pervasive use of software in society.[19] I use the concept of playful capitalism to describe instances in which manifestations of capitalism, from digital to platform to surveillance capitalism, use a play element in a process of value capture.[20] Playful capitalism is the modality of capitalism that uses play as an instrument to perpetuate its logic of value extraction and exploitation.

Playful capitalism has a foundation in what Mark Fisher defined as capitalist realism.[21] This concept describes the social and cultural situation in which capitalism is seen as the only possible economic and political system. In contemporary Western societies, alternatives to capitalism are unthinkable, and therefore cultural, social, and political manifestations all take for granted capital as the foundation for society. In his words, "Capitalism is what is left when beliefs have collapsed at the level of ritual or symbolic elaboration, and all that is left is the consumer-spectator, trudging through the ruins and the relics."[22]

In this atmosphere, Fisher identifies the phenomenon of *reflexive impotence* as defining the attitude of subjects to capital: "they know things are bad, but more than that, they know they can't do anything about it. But that 'knowledge', that reflexivity, is not a passive observation of an already existing state of affairs. It is a self-fulfilling prophecy."[23] Under capitalist realism, there is a surrender, an acknowledgment of the impossibility of an alternative (or the impossibility of not just imagining but also enacting an alternative), and a certain desire for that alternative not to exist: "Capitalist realism . . . entails subordinating oneself to a reality that is infinitely plastic, capable of reconfiguring itself at any moment."[24]

This form of capitalism draws on control that is accepted in the surrender of its subjects to the unescapable logic of capital: "What needs to be kept in mind is *both* that capitalism is a hyper-abstract impersonal structure *and* that it would be nothing without our co-operation."[25] For capitalist realism to exist, the participation of its subject is imperative. "Control only works if you are complicit with it," and therefore a challenge of capitalist realist technologies is to turn devices of and for control into pleasurable instruments of this complicit behavior.[26]

That is the instrumental role of play in a capitalist realist context: to make control and participation into something pleasurable. Capital turns play into an instrument that camouflages reflexive impotence with a false sense of choice. Because play has been traditionally described as an activity based on a voluntary acceptance of rules, instrumentalizing play for the complicity with capital makes it feel like a voluntary action, like acting on a choice where there was no choice.

Fisher is aware that data collection is an essential element of the capitalist world he is describing. *Capitalist Realism* reflects on "machineries of self-surveillance that create and feed the control mechanisms that bind people to capital."[27] Fisher's work can be understood as a psycho-economical reflection on the effects of Srnicek's platform capitalism, which is defined as the particular instantiation of "advanced capitalism [that] came to be centred upon extracting and using a particular kind of raw material: data."[28] Zuboff's notion of surveillance capitalism is akin to platform capitalism: data are extracted from users and commodified.[29] Zuboff's arguments draw from political theory about democracy, a Foucauldian understanding of power and its structures and a regulation-driven perspective on privacy. Srnicek's perspective is more concerned with the effects of platform capitalism and its wars for control of resources. In this view of capitalism, platforms become empires, "owners of the infrastructures of society."[30] The games of empire are no longer only certain video games: they are all forms of playable media that platforms use for extracting data.

Digital platforms benefit from data not just as raw material they can refine and sell but also in a broader range of functions: "They educate and give competitive advantage to algorithms, they enable the coordination and outsourcing of workers, they allow for the optimization and flexibility of productive processes; they make possible the transformation of low-margin goods into high-margin services; and data analysis is itself generative of data, in a virtuous cycle."[31] That is, the extraction of data is essential for the functioning of platform capitalism, even when it's not just the data that become products. In the context of playful capitalism, this is critical because "platforms must deploy a range of tactics to ensure that more and more users come on board and because data extraction must also foster co-operation and complicity with the system to strengthen the notion that there is no alternative to capital."[32]

It is in this context that play is used as an instrument of capital. For platforms to continue their data extraction through instruments of control that declare the inevitability of capitalism, play as a form of agency is a tempting instrument. It allows for a voluntary acceptance of rules that limits the horizon of reflection, is situated in the here-and-now of the play activity, and rewards that submission with transient, often quantifiable pleasures. Fisher already identified that this system "can be characterized without hyperbole as 'market Stalinism.' What late capitalism repeats from Stalinism is just this valuing of symbols of achievement over actual achievement."[33] The technologies of playful capitalism that allow for value capture and data extraction will use play as a way of rewarding compliance with the platform goals of data extraction.

Corporations and platforms that profit from massive data extraction and processing are pioneers in using gamification and other forms of playable media to exert control over their workers. There is an acknowledgment from both platforms and workers that labor under these conditions is repetitive, dehumanizing, and tedious. Adding games and other forms of competitive play is supposed to make the tedium of work less burdening. One well-known case of data-driven gamification of labor in a platform corporation is that of Amazon warehouses.[34]

Amazon is a platform the integrates physical products and a vast infrastructural control over the internet thanks to its Amazon Web Services products. Amazon is one of the engines of platform capitalism, using data extraction and processing across its physical and digital products to increase revenue. Amazon's use of data is not restricted to mining customers to recommend its products or to resell its data: it is also an instrument for the control of its workers in physical warehouses. Amazon's Prime service, which guarantees deliveries within hours of an order in certain parts of the world, depends on the precision of its warehouse workers in filling the orders. The labor conditions of these workers are highly exploitative, with the company allowing them few breaks and actively breaking any attempt to unionize.[35] Geissler's autofictional book *Seasonal Associate* draws a merciless picture of how, in an Amazon warehouse, everything and every*body* are just commodities at the service of commerce.[36]

Although Amazon's general policy is to deny these accusations, the company does not deny that work in its warehouses is tedious and monotonous. At the same time, these tasks need to be performed at speed and with extreme precision to meet the exacting demands of the organization. For these reasons, Amazon started deploying games as instruments to incentivize efficiency and keep workers engaged. Workers in some Amazon warehouses were encouraged, not forced, to play some games in which they would compete with others in fulfilling their tasks. The rewards for performing well in these games are of course not connected to the economic profit of the corporation. Workers who thrive in these games get tokens of appreciation: Amazon-branded gear and occasionally electronics. Worker exploitation thus reaches a new low: workers are not only forced to work in impossible conditions, they are also encouraged to have "fun" by playing games and competing with each other, but the rewards are not even valuable compensation for the profit they generate for the platform.

The idea of finding pleasure in work through play evokes Donald Roy's description of how workers tried to make work more interesting in their "banana time" but crucially ignores one of the conclusions of that research.[37] Roy argued that the creation of social structures in work helped make it more bearable. By structuring the gamification of labor in the warehouse through the use of agonistic, competitive games that have scores and reward individual performance, Amazon also undermines the possibility of collective action as workers may see each other as competitors, not comrades.

According to journalistic reports, the games played in these warehouses are nostalgic reinterpretations of video games classics like *Space Invaders* and *Breakout*, with a visual design connected to the fulfilling of their tasks. For example, Amazon Prime substitutes the bricks for the aliens in a *Breakout* clone. Nostalgia and gaming are used as interfaces that camouflage the ruthlessness of the data-driven exploitation of workers in Amazon's warehouses. Amazon's use of these instruments illustrates how (competitive) games, play, and platform capitalism work so well together: Amazon's lifeblood is the data that articulate its businesses. Workers are part of these data streams, and if they are treated as data points, parts of computational processes, a more efficient extraction of value from their labor will be possible. In order to ameliorate this dehumanizing project and to provide workers with an illusion of freedom and agency, Amazon uses games as interfaces. A platform's workings become a game, and interacting with its data-driven nature becomes a form of play. There is no alternative to the kind of exploitation that Amazon or the other platforms demand; there are only ways of making that exploitation moderately less painful, slightly more entertainment, just a bit more playful.

In the context of platform capitalist realism, play technologies become instruments for control, data extraction, and algorithmic work. Gamification of labor exploitation provides an obvious example of the appropriation of play by predatory platforms. But playful capitalism is more pervasive than this explicit form of play.

Play as Heteromatic Ghost Work

Gamification is an obvious application of play to the workings of capital in the digital age. There are, however, more insidious ways in which platforms are using the ludic to further their data-extractive policies, profiting from labor hidden as play. As new forms of exploitation emerge and new ways of profiting from people take shape, platforms develop original applications of play to seduce "users" into submitting to the platform's premises.

In the first decades of the twenty-first century, artificial intelligence has become one of the star products of platform capitalism. Machine learning techniques that allow for the development of systems that can learn on their own, coupled with the availability of massive amounts of data to train those systems thanks to the digitization of society, have created new data-driven products and possibilities for economic gains. These systems are only as good as the data they are fed. Therefore, platforms have become even hungrier in their acquisition of data from users. The more data they have, the more accurate these algorithms' statistical approximations to reality will be. The closer to reality they are, the easier it will become to eventually rule out workers, from taxi drivers to computer programmers.

The data for these systems require a laborious process of cleaning and preparing. That is a labor-intensive process, leading to the creation of a new type of exploitative work: that of the human-in-the-loop who cleans and tags massive amounts of repetitive data so algorithms can be better trained. Earlier in this book I introduced the concept of ghost work as defined by Gray and Suri: "By design, ghost work attempts to strip a job down to its bare necessities: an assignment and a payday. Designers of on-demand labor platforms assume `users' work independently and autonomously. To them, workers are one piece of the bigger puzzle of how to offer goods and services quickly and efficiently to consumers. Digital labor is a means of collecting data to feed into an algorithm or producing content that is good enough, fast enough to meet an urgent deadline."[38]

In this study of Amazon Mechanical Turk workers, Gray and Suri reveal how the very idea of application programming interfaces (APIs) helps abstract away the human labor involved in the processing of the data required by these artificial intelligence systems.[39] Without ghost work, without the exploitation of humans who have been abstracted away in the engineering of systems, the promises of machine learning cannot take place. And we, the users, cannot or choose not to see this work, the backbone of our experience of "intelligent" software.

Ghost work is a type of exploitative labor that falls under what Ekbia and Nardi have defined as heteromation: "Heteromation extracts economic value from *uncompensated* or *low-wage labor*, inciting participation through an intricate set of mechanisms comprised of social and emotional rewards, monetary compensation, and coercion. Generating this value doesn't cost capital much, yet it summons intelligent human labor from the masses across global networks of billions of nodes." Digital capitalism promises software-driven automatic systems that will make work easier and more efficient. However, those systems have become "a critical means by which control and consent are produced and managed."[40] Generating value this way doesn't cost much capital, yet it summons intelligent human labor from the masses across global networks of billions of nodes."[41] Digital capital profits from the labor of gamers, social media participants, content creators in platforms like YouTube, citizen scientists.

To understand how demeaning and predatory ghost work is, Caroline Sinders and Cade Diehm developed an interactive explanation of the pricing of data classification (figure 6.2). Playing around with that calculator shows that no matter how many tasks are taken, given the current pricing per task in ghost work platforms, workers will barely make minimum wage. I can write that argument, but I recommend engaging with Sinders and Diehm's work to understand the full scale of this economic practices (http://trk.network).

Platform capitalism thrives thanks to heteromatic ghost work: low-wage repetitive work that is abstracted away, hidden behind the alleged benefits of the software systems that it powers: "The person and the person's labor disappear; only the output—the computation—is present, revealing once again the marginal character

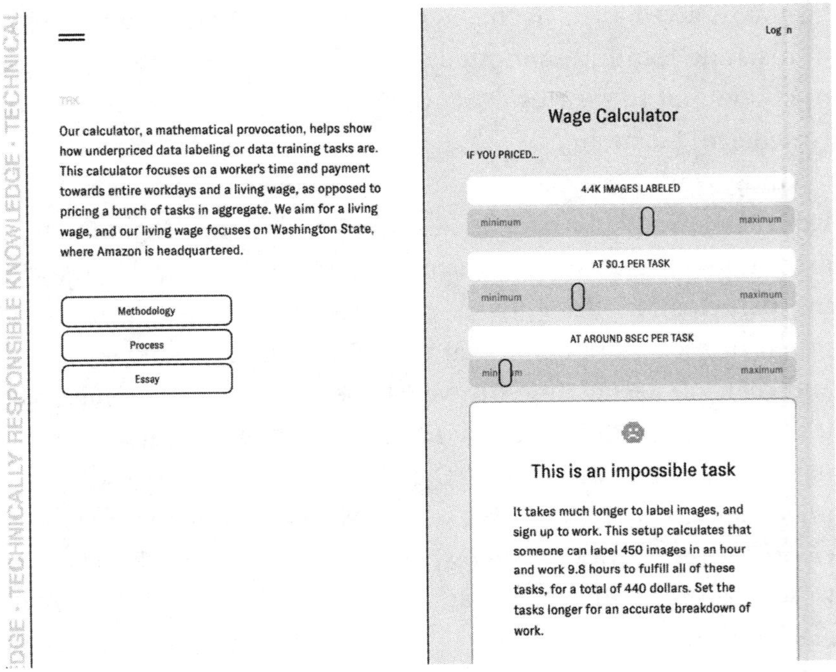

Figure 6.2
trk.network by Caroline Sinders and Cade Diehm. Author's screenshot.

of persons performing heteromatic labor."[42] In order to make this dehumanizing work more endearing, designers of these platforms resort to playfulness to abstract the very nature of heteromatic ghost work. Their argument would be that it cannot be work if you are playing, even if "playing" is just performing repetitive labor. Ekbia and Nardi identify the "play" in social media as a form of labor, as well as the need for stimulation through entertainment these platforms require.[43] In these cases, play is used as an instrument to hide the nature of heteromatic ghost work.

Let's look more closely at an example of heteromation through play. In chapter 3, I wrote about Google's game *Quick, Draw!*[44] To recap on its story, when the game was released, it was initially noticed only within the community of AI researchers, but it soon took off and became an overnight viral sensation. The premise of the game is simple: players receive a prompt commanding them to draw something in under twenty seconds, for example, a bicycle. As players clumsily doodle on their computers, the game is trying to guess what object they are drawing. A round consists of six challenges, and once the round is over, players can see their results, and even inquire how the neural network powering the game figured out from their doodle what the challenge was.

Quick, Draw! is an impressive piece of game design and technology. The neural network that powers it is capable of recognizing a vast number of objects within a few seconds, and playing this game is quite entertaining. The speed with which the drawings are recognized feels magical, furthering the enchantment discourse that is so prevalent around AI and machine learning.[45] *Quick, Draw!* is part of what Google has called AI Experiments (https://experiments.withgoogle.com/collection/ai), playful explorations of what contemporary artificial intelligence can do.

While these AI experiments show the creative promises of computational technology, they also serve another purpose—one that is intertwined with Google's platform capitalist goals. As I have noted, machine learning systems are enormously data hungry, requiring correctly tagged data in order to perform their function properly. Tagging the data is a laborious manual operation that is prone to conscious and unconscious errors.[46] This is the task often given to Mechanical Turkers and other forms of heteromatic ghost workers. but there are other ways of labeling data to create valuable data sets.

Quick, Draw! developers were explicit about the fact that their game was being used to train a neural network model. That relative transparency is admirable, but it also obscures the fact that "training" a machine learning model is not just a fun by-product of playing games: it is tedious work that needs to be done so data sets and algorithms get better. There is an economic incentive in training these data sets, and even if it is fun, playing *Quick, Draw!* is also a form of labor.

Some time after the release of *Quick, Draw!*, Google made public the data set extracted from the game (https://github.com/googlecreativelab/quickdraw-dataset). While the ethos of releasing the data to the public for free deserves praise, the data set itself shows how the apparently harmless game was used to classify and tag doodle data. This process is labor camouflaged as play. Without properly labeled data sets, machine learning is useless. But a well-structured data set can be priceless—a data set that, for example, would power systems that help recognize drawings hastily made with computers. The path to product of this doodle data set is clear, as it can power productivity software, for example.

Players of *Quick, Draw!* were not just "playing": they were performing ghost work. Without their playful engagement with this machine learning program, the system and the data set that can power commercial products would not exist. This is heteromatic ghost work that uses play interactions for the processes of making platform capitalist products possible. There is nothing ethically wrong in playing *Quick, Draw!*, but it should be explicit that this game is more than just "a game." The video game is developed to help train a neural network. That process helps create better data and more efficient algorithms, which are essential for the profit of the corporation behind *Quick, Draw!* Cleaning and perfecting data sets and testing the efficacy of algorithms is time-consuming work. By displacing that work to "players," *Quick, Draw!* proposes a type of ghost play: an activity that looks and feels like playing but in fact is part of a platform for labor extraction.

Gamification wants to make work pleasurable. Forms of heteromatic ghost work like *Quick, Draw!* make digital playthings into labor extraction practices. In this way, they are a more insidious instrumentalization of play, a form of ghost play that hides extraction labor practices under the appearance of games and other playable media. *Quick, Draw!* is naively explicit about this, but the use of playable media to gather data that can be commercialized by platforms is extended everywhere: video games profile users while they play, and therefore they are providing their products for free since it's the data that are valuable.[47] Play-to-earn games, built on blockchain technologies as a way for platforms to centralize the informal economies around games, provide another variation of ghost play. Social media platforms are not just gamified; they draw on lessons from games and play design to make their products more engaging. In the age of data platforms, playable media have become another extractive technology for corporate profit.

Play makes platforms pleasurable and makes workers of all players. The case of *Quick, Draw!* illustrates a way in which play is used as an instrument of capital. This, however, should not be the dismal conclusion of this chapter's reflections. There is more to play and playable media than being an instrument for capitalist realism, and there are reasons to end this book with a note of hope.

World Traveling in Capitalism

In *The Utopia of Rules*, David Graeber writes, "Games allow us our only real experience of a situation where ambiguity is swept away. Everyone knows exactly what the rules are. And not only that, people actually do follow them. And by following them, it is even possible to win! This—along with the fact that unlike in real life, one has submitted oneself to the rules completely voluntarily—is the source of the pleasure. Games, then, are a kind of utopia of rules."[48] These are the games, and the play, that platform capitalism instrumentalizes: a form of engaging with platforms that eliminates ambiguity, rewards actions, and calls for voluntary submission in exchange of pleasure.

Graeber then takes the argument in a different direction: "What ultimately lies behind the appeal of bureaucracy is fear of play."[49] He argues that play is freedom, and that freedom is often at odds with order, rules, and submission to production. Play in this way stands against the rigidness of control and the threats of violence of modern bureaucracies. Drawing on the same tradition of play that informs Schechner's dark play,[50] Graeber defends play as a counterbalance to the forms of order of contemporary capitalism, echoing the anarchist tradition in play studies.[51]

I draw hope from a different place. María Lugones despised the destructive playfulness of Western white men as that of order and competition. That is the "play" used to extract labor and submit people to algorithmic systems. She provides us with an alternative: "The playfulness that gives meaning to our activity includes uncertainty, but in this case the uncertainty is an *openness to surprise*. This is a particular metaphysical attitude that does not expect the world to be neatly packaged, ruly. Rules may fail to explain what we are doing. . . . We may not have rules, and when we do have rules, there are no rules that are to us sacred."[52]

The form of play Lugones advocates for, the one I have adopted in this book, cannot be reduced to an instrument of capital. It is a form of play that acknowledges the existence of other worlds we can travel to and attempt to understand ourselves and others. It is a form of play that wants to meet others and understand them—not conquer them, not extract anything from them, but to be with them, together, in creating worlds. Platform capitalism presents technological development as a desired imperative, one in which we are individually mined for data and playfully encouraged to produce more data and work for the platform. There are no other words in the capitalist realism of platforms.

Lugones's play encourages us to look beyond the logic of quantified pleasures of digital capitalistic playfulness and to find others in worlds where rules are unimportant and what matters is the relation to those others, the loving travel to those worlds. In an interview with *Logic* magazine, Donna Haraway gives play a central role in finding new possibilism: "Through playful engagement with each other, we get a hint about what can still be and learn how to make it stronger."[53] Platform capitalism thrives in reducing the horizon of humanity to the inevitable reality of inescapable capital. It gives a way of meeting others, of learning and identifying their worlds, of acting together in breaking the rules that are given and making other rules. Play is not just the proposal of alternative ideas: it is the exploration of other ideas, acting with others, asserting what can be. This form of world traveling thrives in the possible, breaks the grim realism of capital, and gives possible spaces for other worlds to come to being.

I don't mean to be naive and think that we can end capitalism through play. I also know that the examples in this book, and this book itself, are a consequence of this political and economic context. By the end of the day, we have to pay bills, eat, and even have fun, and that requires being part of this capitalist society. Playing is a way of giving us the biggest "what if" possible: not just to imagine different worlds but to make them come into being. More, even: to let us live in them and let others live in them. Playing software as world traveling, as an appropriation of the entanglement process with artificial agencies that creates worlds, can bring new worlds to fruition. These worlds will not happen if we follow the rules and processes of most software, because most software is a tool for the masters. Playing software is the enactment of other processes, of other rules, so we can meet together, and understand each other, human and animal and artificial, in worlds we create. Playing software can be creating other tools for living in other worlds, with all others.

7 Endings

A driverless car is racing down your street. Suddenly you realize that you are standing in the middle of the lane, and you freeze in terror. In the other lane, an old man has started crossing the street with his grandchild, Damien, whose presence has always made your dog uneasy. The old man and the child are unaware that the car is speeding down the street. The software running the car will have to make a choice, but somebody will have to die (figure 7.1). In what may be your last seconds on earth, you reflect on the fact that maybe the software has been developed in collaboration with the brightest ethical minds in the world, and so if it decides you shall die, there may be a good reason for that.

Or perhaps the driverless car has been trained by overworked software developers using whichever data sets they could put together before the next earnings call. Or worse, some of those data might have been harvested from playing some interactive scenarios, like those proposed by the project Moral Machine (moralmachine.net).

In this project, users (players) are offered different scenarios in which a self-driving car needs to make a decision in a scenario similar to that I just described. The results of the choices are presented

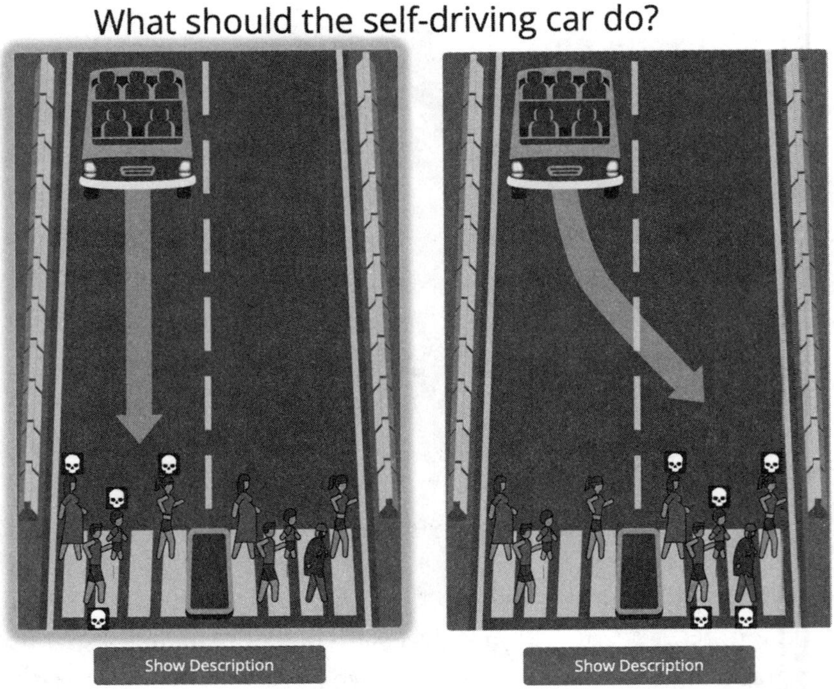

Figure 7.1
Helping cars make decisions. Author's screenshot.

as continua that resemble those evaluations of moral character from video games like *Fallout* or *Knights of the Old Republic*. Essentially, Moral Machine is an interactive version of Philippa Foot's famous trolley problem, which artificial intelligence engineers use to address all kinds of ethical dilemmas that arise from the presence of artificial agents in our lifeworlds.[1]

In the use of these interactive dilemmas to teach people (and maybe even train AIs) to "behave ethically," we can see another form of play helping us make sense of software. The dilemmas in Moral Machine are playful interactions that should let developers understand the potential ethical solutions that people would apply to the challenge of self-driving cars. Once again, play is a way to relate to the alien agency of software. Much as in the case of Animojis, play is used here to help us understand how software agents act and how our actions should be in the entanglement with these agents. That is, these playable examples teach us how to live together with driverless cars.

This creates an ethical problem. No, not the driverless car—after all, the ethical solution to the driverless car is easy: we should not let cars drive themselves. The problem is that these playful dilemmas treat technology as inevitable and model human agency as something that needs to relate to that inevitability. Specifically in the case of AI, it seems that our only way to address AI is to learn to live with it. The struggle to make AI recognize people of color and women shows how flawed, technically and morally, this software is. And yet nothing is stopping us from adding more and more AI to the world and making more and more forms of playable engagement with it so we can digest what it is making us become.

That is the key ethical challenge that software poses: it can change our agency. Software may be programmed so we can be computable only in certain ways. This has an effect on the world, comparable to when robots are deployed on factory floors and their presence changes the physical environment of the production chain to accommodate them. This process is called "enveloping," and we can say that in the information age, we envelop the world and ourselves to be able to live together with software. And to make that process more livable, we use play as a way of making this entanglement with software pleasurable and fun. We don't question whether we should have driverless cars, or face recognition on mobile devices, or microphones connected to natural language processing systems installed in our homes. What we question is how to make those inevitable signs of progress more fun. Play is deployed to make the apparent inevitability of software more palatable.

But play can be more than an instrument for technological determinism. For Lugones, play and playfulness are inevitably ethical. There is an ethos of playing as world traveling. Huizinga famously situated play outside morality, and for decades, the discussion of the ethics of play has navigated the tension between the fact that players are moral beings and playing allows for the exploration of conventions in morality. Playing software is also situated in that tension, but thanks to Lugones's theory, there is a way of actually sketching an ethics of play in the information age.

Playing software is a meeting of agencies, an entanglement of the biological and the digital. Understanding that meeting as world traveling implies that in the play interface, agents need to negotiate how they relate to each other. Lugones is adamant in her arguments about playfulness: world traveling needs to be loving, it needs to be able to acknowledge others as well as help us shape our own self. World traveling in play implies seeing others, negotiating agencies, being allowed to create that world together.

This should not throw away the idea of the pleasures of submitting to rules. This idea of loving world traveling means that even when agents reduce their agency, submit to rules, *do what they are told*, they do so voluntarily, fully understanding the reasons and the ways in which that submission can be stopped. Submitting to others is also a recognition of others' agency, and voluntarily submitting others is also a recognition of the other.

This is the essence of Lugones's ethos and what should be at the core of the ethics of playing software: the meeting of agencies needs to be established on a loving understanding of all agents involved. Loving is the right word because it establishes that playing is based on respect, acknowledgement, and the wide spectrum of forms of loving biology and the artificial allow. It is not an *ethics*, but an *ethos*, a driving principle that we can then formulate into different ethical discourses.

I like to think of playing software as a form of creative stewardship.[2] Playing is always in tension between order and chaos, and maintaining order in play is not trivial. Loving world traveling requires the stewardship of the worlds we are given, but it is open for a creative engagement, for adding the personal, expressive mark of agencies human and nonhuman.

The moralmachine.net project falls short of becoming a loving way of playing software, because it takes for granted that driverless cars are inevitable. It does not ask us to meet with them; it asks us to submit to them. The way it asks this question is playful, no doubt. But it is not playing software, because there's never a meeting point between the software and the other agents, human and animal, that live in the same world. The data gathered through this form of playable interaction might end up feeding a system that we, the players of those dilemmas, have never had a way to relate to. It is a form of play, but it's not playing software, because there is no meeting of agencies to create a new world. AI is imposed on the world, other agents need to adapt, and that adaptation is explained with playable dilemmas.

Economic interests and the complexities of technology may serve as arguments to shield these technologies from play. Maybe technology is no laughing matter, no loving matter, and we should let it be the work of the clever men of science. But we may also just play with it anyway. Part of the privilege of art is to be able to play even in forbidden domains. Therefore, if we want to think about playing software with technologies that seem too serious to be played with, we need to see where rules are broken, where there's laughter, where artists are playing software.

For example, blockchain will be the future for ledger-based transactions until the earth's ecosystems collapse, partially because of the increased energy consumption of this technology. Blockchain technology has promised to make fishing and agriculture more sustainable, as well as legal contracts more clear and enforceable. However, at the point of this writing, its most popular application has been the creation of cryptocurrencies of variable worth and value.

However, artists know better. And what better use of the blockchain than making dick pics accountable? In the art project NFT the DP (http://nftthedp.com), Zoe Scaman created the most useful application of blockchain I know of. Riding on the 2021 craze for blockchain-based nonfungible tokens (NFTs) that promised that even digital art could be unique and individual, Scaman decided to give a twist to the concept of unique digital files.

If anybody receives an unwelcome dick picture, they can use the website nftthedp.com to upload it, mint it as an NFT in the blockchain, give it a price, and then publish it. The picture will be in the blockchain, for everybody in the world to see. And the only way to get rid of it would be to purchase the item by using actual money and then send it to a specific address that is on the website so it can be deleted.

NFT the DP appropriates one of the core values of blockchain, the capacity it has to make more or less unique even digital elements, and turns it on its head to use it as an instrument to playfully punish those who send unsolicited dick pics. This mischievously fun little project actually understands the ethos of world traveling. Blockchain technology might be fascinating, but so far it has been implemented in ways that appeal only to those who believe in a better world through technology. NFT the DP engages with what blockchain can do with its agency and creates a shared world that is the opposite of what blockchain worlds promise: a gathering of laughing agencies, a less serious take on what technology is and what it can do, or what it does to us.

But I also need to address another purpose of this book. I was writing this book when a world started to end. The unstoppable events linked to climate change were starting to take place. There were floods, storms, hurricanes, waterless winters, and parched-dried summers. Australia was—is?—on fire. The sixth mass extinction is well underway. The seasons are vanishing while many species will never see the incoming wasteland. The world as I've always known it, the world in which this book makes sense, might not last for long. Whatever world will take place after this one ends will be shaped by other cultures. People might rise to the challenge and realize that we cannot be the predators of our planet. Or maybe fascism and feudalism will become allies in a forever looping dark age.

What is the point of writing about play and technology when a world is ending? What is the place of this book in this time and the times ahead? If you are a reader from a future where reading makes sense and is possible, what can you possibly make of this book? What difference does it make to write a theory book about the role of play in shaping software culture when software culture might be a culprit in its own demise?

One easy answer, the one we all want to hear, is that we need to understand play because play is important for people. I can list here the many ways that historically we have thought about how important play is, how we thought it to be revolutionary, critical for learning, and a cornerstone of the future. How play can save us only if we all play.

But that is not true. Play cannot save us more than anything else can save us.

Why study play, then? Why read this book? I have no satisfying answer, but to say that if we want to understand people, if we want to understand the technologies that helped develop the end of this world, we need to understand play. This is not a book that gives answers. This is a book that wants readers to question.

Why do we use play to make sense of software? What does it mean when big corporations promote their products as play or playful? What do we gain and what do we lose when our relations to the world of computational things are shaped by play? Play promises us freedom, but does it deliver it, or does it enslave us? Play promises us pleasure, but at what price, and who is allowed to have pleasure? Is the software that wants us to play just amusing us while we become the last of the extractable goods, valuable data siphoned out while we watch the world burn?

Or is play actually something positive? Is play allowing us to imagine and act possibilities different from those inscribed in the rules of software? Are the worlds we create through computational media emancipatory worlds? Are they open to act in ways that were not there before? Is the play of software the imagination of the possibilities, the liberation of what worlds we can conceive thanks to the alien agencies of computational media?

Play can remind us that we are not the machines we make, that we are not on any manifest path to any technological destiny, that not every problem requires a technical solution. Play reminds us that this world is *ours to make* but also *ours to unmake*—that we can create all kinds of rules to shape who we are and what we think the world is, but that we can also break them. Play reminds us that we can imagine and live in fantastical worlds, but also that inside every person there is an oppressor, and that seeking the pleasure in others' pain is play as much as it is learning from others how to say new words or express new feelings.

This world ends because we collectively fell in love with technologies, because we thought we could master and control them, because we set rules and maybe thought that everything was a game, the world our playground. So maybe this book can be read as a cautionary tale: because play helps us make sense of technology and of ourselves, we never saw this end game. Play, always in tension between creation and destruction, between order and chaos, between rules and cheats, gave us meanings for this world we lived in, but it also contributed to the end of this world.

I am, however, an optimist. Playing is not just creating worlds; it's living in them. It's not just imagining possibilities; it's making them happen. Even if those possibilities are short-lived, bound to transient fun and pleasure of playing, we can say they have existed. And because they have existed, we know they can exist. Brian Sutton-Smith once quipped that the opposite of play is not work but depression. I'd add that the opposite of playing is nihilism.

This ethos requires us to denounce the instrumentalization of play, the corruption of play as an instrument for easing the end of these worlds. It also requires us to imagine new ways of making software agents we can relate to, we can entangle with. In exchange, playing software promises us that a dying world may not be inevitable, that we can dare to create new worlds, and keep playing together, having fun.

I end this book with a defense of fun. I used to be highly skeptical of the concept of fun because I distrusted a concept that could not be formally defined. And yet the more I looked at the way playing software can be used to imagine and enact possible better worlds, the more I saw fun and laughter everywhere. So I learned that we need fun, or, as David Graeber put it, "What is the point if we can't have fun?"[3]

So what is the point of fun in playing software? Fun is vague and difficult to define, and it varies from person to person and from culture to culture and from time to time. Fun is elusive, but we chase because it does something to us, with us, to others, and to the world that we simply need. Fun is liminal and ambiguous because it is not *something*.

Having fun is a shared experience, a negotiation of joys and pleasures that requires an effort and occasionally will be impossible to explain. A fun entanglement requires an agreement, a mode of respect of the others we're having fun with. And fun is essential in playing software because it implies an escape from the regimented world of processes and duties and control. Fun is breaking away from what shall happen and enjoying the surprise and the pleasures of new arrangements. Fun is searching for desirable possibilities beyond what is given as fact, as the way things are, as the way things have been.

Fun can be a horrible thing too because it can be fun to make others miserable. As I argued in chapters 5 and 6, fun can be used to facilitate technologies of oppression. We have to live with the fact that fun is not always fun *for all*. And that's why, again, Lugones's ethos is critical to not only understand but also evaluate the role of playing software in the information age. Fun is the outcome of creating worlds that are open to others, that deny toxic agencies and foster new forms of togetherness. Fun happens in worlds where we can explore others and ourselves.

Playing software is an ethos, a practice that is always absolutely of moral nature. Play is not separate from the world or alien to ethics. Playing is creating worlds, and doing so with an ethos. The cultures that emerge from playing software are subject to ethical scrutiny because they are the result of world making, of the creation of subjectivities, of telling humans, animals, and software who they are, what to do, how to be.

We should be critical when playing software. We should always think about the artificial agencies we meet, how they entangle with us, which worlds are then created and for whom. But we should also have some fun. The information age wants desperately to be the age of command and control of humans and animals and the environment and itself. Playing software makes ambitions relative. It entangles us with these alien agencies; it lets us create worlds, experience that there are other worlds we could create and that creating them should ultimately be fun for all. Playing software should not be a matter of exchanges of information in regimes of control. It should not be a transactional activity but a relational one: a way of being and becoming in a world shared with multiple others while having fun.

Notes

Chapter 0

1. Bethesda Game Studios, *Fallout 3* (Bethesda Softworks, 2008); Blizzard Entertainment, *World of Warcraft* (Blizzard Entertainment, 2004).

2. Megacrit, *Slay the Spire* (Humble Bundle, 2019).

3. Bruno Latour, *Reassembling the Social: An Introduction to Actor-Network-Theory* (Oxford: Oxford University Press, 2008); Janet Vertesi and David Ribes, *DigitalSTS: A Field Guide for Science and Technology Studies* (Princeton: Princeton University Press, 2019).

4. Bruno Latour, "Where Are the Missing Masses? The Sociology of a Few Mundane Artifacts," in *Shaping Technology/Building Society: Studies in Sociotechnical Change*, ed. Wiebe E. Bijker and John Law (Cambridge, MA: MIT Press, 1992), 225–258; Manuel DeLanda, *A New Philosophy of Society: Assemblage Theory and Social Complexity* (London: Bloomsbury, 2019).

5. Ed Finn, *What Algorithms Want: Imagination in the Age of Computing* (Cambridge, MA: MIT Press, 2017); Nick Seaver, "Knowing Algorithms," in *DigitalSTS: A Field Guide for Science and Technology Studies*, ed. Janet Vertesi and David Ribes (Princeton: Princeton University Press, 2019), 412–422.

6. Mark Coeckelbergh, *Moved by Machines: Performance Metaphors and Philosophy of Technology* (London: Routledge, 2019).

7. Jessa Lingel and Kate Crawford, "'Alexa, Tell Me about Your Mother': The History of the Secretary and the End of Secrecy," *Catalyst: Feminism, Theory, Technoscience* 6, no. 1 (2020): 1–25.

8. Byron Reeves and Clifford Nass, *The Media Equation: How People Treat Computers, Television, and New Media Like Real People and Places* (New York: Cambridge University Press, 1996).

9. Deborah Lupton, *The Quantified Self* (New York: Polity Press, 2016); Dawn Nafus and Jamie Sherman, "Big Data, Big Questions| This One Does Not Go Up to 11: The Quantified Self Movement as an Alternative Big Data Practice," *International Journal of Communication* 8 (2014): 1784–1794; Jennifer R. Whitson, "Gaming the Quantified Self," *Surveillance and Society* 11, no. 1/2 (May 27, 2013): 163–176.

10. Tilde Bekker, Janienke Sturm, and Berry Eggen, "Designing Playful Interactions for Social Interaction and Physical Play," *Personal and Ubiquitous Computing* 14, no. 5 (December 17, 2009): 385–396; Sebastian Deterding, "Make-Believe in Gameful and Playful Design," in *Digital Make-Believe*, ed. Phil Turner and J. Tuomas Harviainen (Basel: Springer, 2016), 101–124; John Ferrara, *Playful Design: Creating Game Experiences in Everyday Interfaces* (New York: Rosenfeld Media, 2012); Amy B. Woszczynski, Philip L. Roth, and Albert H. Segars, "Exploring the Theoretical Foundations of Playfulness in Computer Interactions," *Computers in Human Behavior* 18, no. 4 (2002): 369–388; Peta Wyeth et al., "The Internet of Playful Things," in *Proceedings of the 2015 Annual Symposium, SIGCHI, ACM Special Interest Group on Computer-Human Interaction* (New York: ACM, 2015), 821–826.

11. Gaby David and Carolina Cambre, "Screened Intimacies: Tinder and the Swipe Logic," *Social Media + Society* 2, no. 2 (January 1, 2016); Maria B. Garda and Veli-Matti Karhulahti, "Let's Play Tinder! Aesthetics of a Dating App," *Games and Culture* 16, no. 2 (2021): 248–261.

12. Stephanie Boluk and Patrick LeMieux, *Metagaming: Playing, Competing, Spectating, Cheating, Trading, Making, and Breaking Videogames* (Minnesota: University of Minnesota Press, 2017).

13. Eric Gordon and Gabriel Mugar, *Meaningful Inefficiencies: Civic Design in an Age of Digital Expediency* (Oxford: Oxford University Press, 2020); Bernard Suits, *The Grasshopper: Games, Life and Utopia* (Toronto: University of Toronto Press, 1978).

Chapter 1

1. Stephanie Boluk and Patrick LeMieux, *Metagaming: Playing, Competing, Spectating, Cheating, Trading, Making, and Breaking Videogames* (Minneapolis: University of Minnesota Press, 2017), 8.

2. Luciano Floridi, *The Ethics of Information* (Oxford: Oxford University Press, 2015). Jean-François Lyotard, *The Postmodern Condition: A Report on Knowledge* (Minneapolis: University of Minnesota Press, 1984).

3. Luciano Floridi, *The Philosophy of Information* (Oxford: Oxford University Press, 2013).

4. Nick Couldry and José van Dijck, "Researching Social Media As If the Social Mattered," *Social Media+Society* 1, no. 2 (September 22, 2015): 1–7; Robert W. Gehl, "The Case for Alternative Social Media," *Social Media+Society* 1, no. 2 (September 22, 2015): 1–12; Lee Humphreys, *The Qualified Self: Social Media and the Accounting of Everyday Life* (Cambridge, MA: MIT Press, 2018); Shannon Vallor, "Flourishing on Facebook: Virtue Friendship and New Social Media," *Ethics and Information Technology* 14, no. 3 (January 8, 2011): 185–199.

5. Katriina Heljakka, "Contemporary Toys, Adults and Creative Material Culture: From Wow to Flow to Glow," in *Materiality and Popular Culture*, ed. Anna Malinowska and Karolina Lebek (New York: Routledge, 2016), 237–249.

6. Christena Nippert-Eng, "Boundary Play," *Space and Culture* 8, no. 3 (August 1, 2005): 302–324.

7. Noah Wardrip-Fruin, *Expressive Processing: Digital Fictions, Computer Games, and Software Studies* (Cambridge, MA: MIT Press, 2009).

8. Robinhood Markets, *Robinhood* (Robinhood Markets, 2015).

9. Martin Pichlmair and Mads Johansen, "Designing Game Feel: A Survey," *IEEE Transactions on Games*) 2021), doi: 10.1109/TG.2021.3072241.

10. Jacques Ehrmann, Cathy Lewis, and Phil Lewis, "Homo Ludens Revisited," *Yale French Studies*, no. 41 (1968): 31–57; Margaret Carlisle Duncan, "Play Discourse and the Rhetorical Turn: A Semiological Analysis of Homo Ludens," *Play and Culture* 1 (1988): 28–42.

11. Valerie Frissen et al., eds., "Homo Ludens 2.0: Play, Media, and Identity," in *Playful Identities*, ed. Valerie Frissen, Sybille Lammes, Michiel de Lange, Jos de Mul, and Joost Raessens (Amsterdam: Amsterdam University Press, 2015), 9–50.

12. Sherry Turkle, *Life on the Screen: Identity in the Age of the Internet* (New York: Simon & Schuster, 1997); Brenda Laurel, *Computers as Theatre* (Boston: Addison-Wesley, 1993).

13. Thomas S. Henricks, *Play and the Human Condition* (Urbana: University of Illinois Press, 2016).

14. David Graeber, *The Utopia of Rules: On Technology, Stupidity, and the Secret Joys of Bureaucracy* (San Francisco: Melville House, 2016), 192.

15. María Lugones, "Playfulness, 'World'-Travelling, and Loving Perception," *Hyapatia* 2, no. 2 (1987), 3–19.

16. Lugones, 15.

17. Lugones, 9–12.

18. Lugones, 10.

19. Lugones, 10.

20. Lugones, 11.

21. Lugones, 14.

22. Lugones, 14–15.

23. Lugones, 17.

24. Hans Georg Gadamer, *Truth and Method* (London: Continuum, 2004).

25. Lugones, "Playfulness, 'World'-Travelling, and Loving Perception," 17.

26. Jaakko Stenros, "Playfulness, Play, and Games: A Constructionist Ludology Approach" (PhD diss., Tampere University Press, 2015), http://tampub.uta.fi/handle/10024/96986; Sebastian Deterding, "The Game Frame: Systemizing a Goffmanian Approach to Video Game Theory," paper presented at "Breaking New Ground: Innovation in Games, Play, Practice, and Theory," the 2009 Digital Games Research Association (DiGRA) conference, London, UK, September 1–4, 2009, http://www.digra.org/wp-content/uploads/digital-library/09287.43112.pdf.

27. Miguel Angel Sicart and Irina Shklovski, "'Pataphysical Software: (Ridiculous) Technological Solutions for Imaginary Problems," in *Proceedings of the 2020 ACM Designing Interactive Systems Conference* (New York: Association for Computing Machinery, 2020), 1859–1871.

28. Christopher Frauenberger, "Entanglement HCI The Next Wave?," *ACM Transactions in Computer-Human Interaction* 27, no. 1 (November 2019): 1–27; Donna Haraway, *Manifestly Haraway* (Minneapolis: University of Minnesota Press, 2016); N. Katherine Hayles, *My Mother Was a Computer: Digital Subjects and Literary Text* (Chicago: University of Chicago Press, 2005).

29. Diana H. Coole and Samantha Frost, *New Materialisms: Ontology, Agency, and Politics* (Durham: Duke University Press, 2010).

30. Douglas Wilson, "Designing for the Pleasures of Disputation-or-How to Make Friends by Trying to Kick Them!" (PhD diss., Copenhagen, IT University of Copenhagen, 2012), http://doougle.net/phd/Designing_for_the_Pleasures_of_Disputation.pdf; Bernie DeKoven, *The Well-Played Game* (Cambridge, MA: MIT Press, 2013).

31. C. Thi Nguyen, *Games: Agency as Art* (Oxford: Oxford University Press, 2020).

32. Miguel Sicart, *The Ethics of Computer Games* (Cambridge, MA: MIT Press, 2009).

33. Mark Coeckelbergh, *Moved by Machines: Performance Metaphors and Philosophy of Technology* (London: Routledge, 2019).

34. Christena Nippert-Eng, "Boundary Play," *Space and Culture* 8, no. 3 (August 1, 2005), 304, 319.

35. Rune Klevjer, "Enter the Avatar: The Phenomenology of Prosthetic Telepresence in Computer Games," in *The Philosophy of Computer Games*, ed. John Richard Sageng, Hallvard Fossheim, and Tarjei Mandt Larsen (Dordrecht: Springer Netherlands, 2012), 17–38.

36. Susanna Paasonen, *Many Splendored Things: Thinking Sex and Play* (Cambridge, MA: MIT Press, 2018).

37. Jacob Johanssen, "Gaming–Playing on Social Media: Using the Psychoanalytic Concept of 'Playing' to Theorize User Labour on Facebook," *Information, Communication and Society* 21, no. 9 (September 2, 2018): 1204–1218.

38. Donna Haraway, "A Giant Bumptious Litter: Donna Haraway on Truth, Technology, and Resisting Extinction," *Logic Magazine*, December 7, 2019, https://logicmag.io/nature/a-giant-bumptious-litter/.

39. Philip Agre, *Computation and Human Experience* (Cambridge, MA: Cambridge University Press, 1997); Warren Sack, *The Software Arts* (Cambridge, MA: MIT Press, 2019).

40. Luciano Floridi, *The Philosophy of Information* (Oxford: Oxford University Press, 2013); Olga Goriunova, "The Digital Subject: People as Data as Persons," *Theory, Culture & Society* 36, no. 6 (2019): 125–145.

41. Luciano Floridi, "Harmonising *Physis* and *Techne*: The Mediating Role of Philosophy," *Philosophy and Technology* 24 (2011): 1–3.

42. Safiya Umoja Noble, *Algorithms of Oppression: How Search Engines Reinforce Racism* (New York: NYU Press, 2018).

43. Joseph Weizenbaum, *Computer Power and Human Reason: From Judgement to Calculation* (San Francisco: Freeman, 1994), 213.

44. Frank Pasquale, *The Black Box Society: The Secret Algorithms That Control Money and Information* (Cambridge, MA: Harvard University Press, 2015); Ed Finn, *What Algorithms Want: Imagination in the Age of Computing* (Cambridge, MA: MIT Press, 2017).

45. Joseph Weizenbaum, *Computer Power and Human Reason: From Judgment to Calculation* (San Francisco: Freeman, 1994), 28

46. Weizenbaum, 115

47. Weizenbaum, 112.

48. Irina Shklovski et al., "Leakiness and Creepiness in App Space: Perceptions of Privacy and Mobile App Use," in *Proceedings of the SIGCHI Conference on Human Factors in Computing Systems* (New York: ACM, 2014), 2347–2356.

49. Kate Crawford and Vladan Joler, "Anatomy of an AI System," accessed May 8, 2019, http://www.anatomyof.ai.

50. Bonnie Ruberg, *Video Games Have Always Been Queer* (New York: NYU Press, 2019); Bonnie Ruberg and Adrienne Shaw, *Queer Game Studies* (Minneapolis: University of Minnesota Press, 2017).

51. Donna Haraway, *Staying with the Trouble: Making Kin in the Chthulucene* (Durham: Duke University Press, 2016).

52. David Graeber, "What's the Point If We Can't Have Fun?," *Baffler*, January 2014, https://thebaffler.com/salvos/whats-the-point-if-we-cant-have-fun.

53. Aaron Trammell, "Torture, Play, and the Black Experience," *GAME: The Italian Journal of Game Studies* 8, no. 9 (2020), https://www.gamejournal.it/torture-play/.

54. C. Thi Nguyen, *Games: Agency as Art* (Oxford: Oxford University Press, 2020).

55. Stenros, "Playfulness, Play, and Games."

Chapter 2

1. Cindy Poremba, "Critical Potential on the Brink of the Magic Circle," paper presented at "Situated Play," the 2007 Digital Games Research Association (DiGRA) conference, Tokyo, Japan, September 24–28, 2007, http://www.digra.org/wp-content/uploads/digital-library/07311.42117.pdf; Mia Consalvo, "There Is No Magic Circle," *Games and Culture* 4, no. 4 (October 1, 2009): 408–417; Johan Huizinga, *Homo Ludens: A Study of the Play-Element in Culture* (London: Beacon Press, 1971).

2. Erving Goffman, *Frame Analysis: An Essay on the Organization of Experience* (Cambridge, MA: Harvard University Press, 1974).

3. Peter-Paul Verbeek, *What Things Do* (University Park: Pennsylvania State University Press, 2006); Peter-Paul Verbeek, "Expanding Mediation Theory," *Foundations of Science* 17, no. 4 (October 8, 2011): 391–395; Robert Rosenberger, "The Sudden Experience of the Computer," *AI and SOCIETY* 24, no. 2 (March 3, 2009): 173–180; Robert Rosenberger, "Multistability and the Agency of Mundane Artifacts: From Speed Bumps to Subway Benches," *Human Studies* 37, no. 3 (July 5, 2014): 369–392; Robert Rosenberger, "The Importance of Generalized Bodily Habits for a Future World of Ubiquitous Computing," *AI and Society* 28, no. 3 (February 21, 2012): 289–296; Christian Ulrik Andersen and Søren Pold, *The Metainterface: The Art of Platforms, Cities, and Clouds* (Cambridge, MA: MIT Press, 2018); Paul Dourish, "Seeing like an Interface," in *Proceedings of the Nineteenth Australasian Conference on Computer-Human Interaction* (New York: ACM, 2007), 1–8; Alexander R Galloway, *The Interface Effect* (New York: Polity Press, 2012); Brendan Keogh, *A Play of Bodies* (Cambridge, MA: MIT Press, 2018).

4. Vilém Flusser, *Post-History* (Minneapolis: University of Minnesota Press, 2013); Friedrich A. Kittler, *Discourse Networks 1800/1900* (Stanford: Stanford University Press, 2007).

5. Siefried Zieliski, Peter Weibel, and Daniel Irrgang, eds., *Flusseriana. An Intellectual Toolbox* (Minneapolis: Univocal, 2015), 236.

6. Alexander R. Galloway, *The Interface Effect* (New York: Polity Press, 2012), 14.

7. Lucy Suchman, *Human–Machine Reconfigurations: Plans and Situated Actions* (Cambridge University Press, 2007); Julie E. Cohen, *Configuring the Networked Self* (New Haven, CT: Yale University Press, 2012).

8. Michel de Certeau and Steven Rendall, *The Practice of Everyday Life* (Berkeley: University of California Press, 1984).

9. Henri Lefebvre, *Critique of Everyday Life: The One-Volume Edition* (London: Verso, 2014).

10. Brendan Keogh, *A Play of Bodies* (Cambridge, MA: MIT Press, 2018); Stephanie Boluk and Patrick LeMieux, *Metagaming: Playing, Competing, Spectating, Cheating, Trading, Making, and Breaking Videogames* (Minneapolis: University of Minnesota Press, 2017).

11. Sonia Fizek, "Automated State of Play: Rethinking Anthropocentric Rules of the Game," *Digital Culture and Society* 4, no. 1 (2018): 201–214; Seth Giddings, *Gameworlds: Virtual Media and Children's Everyday Play* (London: Bloomsbury Press, 2016); Bart Simon, "Geek Chic," *Games and Culture* 2, no. 3 (July 1, 2007): 175–193.

12. Gina Neff and Dawn Nafus, *Self-Tracking* (Cambridge, MA: MIT Press, 2016); Katta Spiel and Kathrin Gerling, "The Surrogate Body in Play," in *Proceedings of the Annual Symposium on Computer-Human Interaction in Play* (New York: ACM, 2019), 397–411.

13. Trevor Paglen, "Invisible Images: Your Pictures Are Looking at You," *Architectural Design* 89, no. 1 (2019): 22–27.

14. Ruha Benjamin, *Race after Technology: Abolitionist Tools for the New Jim Code* (Medford, MA: Polity Press, 2019); Catherine D'Ignazio and Lauren F. Klein, *Data Feminism* (Cambridge, MA: MIT Press, 2020); Safiya Noble, *Algorithms of Oppression: How Search Engines Reinforce Racism* (New York: NYU Press: 2018).

15. This article by James Vincent in The Verge provides some further details on the image outage and its results: https://www.theverge.com/2019/7/3/20681231/facebook-outage-image-tags-captions-ai-machine-learning-revealed.

16. Eric Gordon and Gabriel Mugar, *Meaningful Inefficiencies: Civic Design in an Age of Digital Expediency* (Oxford: Oxford University Press, 2020).

17. Alexander Campolo and Kate Crawford, "Enchanted Determinism: Power without Responsibility in Artificial Intelligence," *Engaging Science, Technology, and Society* 6 (January 8, 2020): 3.

18. Miguel Sicart, "Defining Game Mechanics," *Game Studies* 8, no. 2 (2008).

19. Sherry Turkle, *Life on the Screen: Identity in the Age of the Internet* (New York: Simon & Schuster, 1997); David Sudnow, *Pilgrim in the Microworld* (New York: Warner Books, 1983); Brenda Laurel, *Computers as Theatre*, 2nd ed. (Boston: Addison-Wesley, 1993); N. Katherine Hayles, *My Mother Was a Computer: Digital Subjects and Literary Text* (Chicago: University of Chicago Press, 2005); Janet H. Murray, *Hamlet on the Holodeck: The Future of Narrative in Cyberspace* (New York: Free Press, 1997); Celia Pearce, "Productive Play: Game Culture from the Bottom Up," *Games and Culture* 1, no. 1 (January 1, 2006): 17–24.

20. Suchman, *Human–Machine Reconfigurations*.

21. Keogh, *A Play of Bodies*; Sudnow, *Pilgrim in the Microworld*.

22. Subset Games, *Into the Breach* (Subset Games, 2018). Electronic Arts, *FIFA* (Electronic Arts, 1993).

23. Sid Meier, *Civilization* (MicroProse, 1991).

24. Mike Cook and Simon Colton, "Multi-Faceted Evolution of Simple Arcade Games," in *Proceedings of the 2011 IEEE Conference on Computational Intelligence and Games* (Piscataway, NJ: IEEE, 2011), 289–296; Mike Cook et al., "General Analytical Techniques for Parameter-Based Procedural Content Generators," in *Proceedings of the 2019 IEEE Conference on Game* (Piscataway, NJ: IEEE, 2019), 1–8; Tony Veale and Michael Cook, *Twitterbots: Making Machines That Make Meaning* (Cambridge, MA: MIT Press, 2018); Gillian Smith, "What Do We Value in Procedural Content Generation?," in *Proceedings of the International Conference on the Foundations of Digital Games* (New York: Association for Computing Machinery, 2017), 69:1–69:2; Gillian Smith, "Understanding Procedural Content Generation: A Design-Centric Analysis of the Role of PCG in Games," in *Proceedings of the SIGCHI Conference on Human Factors in Computing Systems* (New York: Association for Computing Machinery, 2014), 917–926.

25. David Braben and Ian Bell, *Elite*, 1984, Michael Toy et al., *Rogue*, 1980; Derek Yu, *Spelunky* (Mossmouth LLC, 2008).

26. C. Thi Nguyen, *Games: Agency as Art* (Oxford: Oxford University Press, 2020).

27. Nguyen, Games.

28. Vectorpark, *Feed the Head* (Vectorpark, 2007).

29. A. Galloway, *Uncomputable: Play and Politics in the Long Digital Age* (London: Verso Books, 2021).

30. Roger Caillois, *Man, Play and Games* (Urbana: University of Illinois Press, 2001).

31. Neil Postman, *Amusing Ourselves to Death: Public Discourse in the Age of Show Business* (London: Penguin Books, 2005).

Chapter 3

1. Miguel Sicart, "Playthings," Games and Culture 17, no. 1: 140–155.

2. Diana H. Coole and Samantha Frost, *New Materialisms: Ontology, Agency, and Politics* (Durham: Duke University Press, 2010).

3. Anne Dippel and Sonia Fizek, "Ludification of Culture," in *The Significance of Play and Games in Everyday Practices of the Digital Era*, ed. Gertraud Koch (Abington: Routledge, 2017), 276–292; Sonia Fizek, "Automated State of Play: Rethinking Anthropocentric Rules of the Game," *Digital Culture and Society* 4, no. 1 (2018): 201–214; Sonia Fizek, "Interpassivity and the Joy of Delegated Play in Idle Games," *Transactions of the Digital Games Research Association* 3, no. 3 (April 30, 2018): 137–163; Cameron Kunzelman, *The Nonhuman Lives of Videogames* (Atlanta: Georgia State University, 2014); Connor McKeown, "Playing with Materiality: An Agential-Realist Reading of SethBling's Super Mario World Code-Injection," *Information, Communication and Society* 21, no. 9 (2018): 1234–1245.

4. Seth Giddings, "A 'Pataphysics Engine," *Games and Culture* 2, no. 4 (October 1, 2007): 392–404; Giddings, *Gameworlds: Virtual Media and Children's Everyday Play* (London: Bloomsbury Press, 2016); Simon, "Geek Chic," *Games and Culture* 2, no. 3 (2007): 175–193; Bart Simon, "Unserious," *Games and Culture* 12, no. 6 (2017): 605–618.

5. Thomas Apperley and Darshana Jayemanne, "Game Studies' Material Turn," *Westminster Papers in Communication and Culture* 9, no. 1 (October 1, 2012): 5–25.

6. Eugen Fink, Ute Saine, and Thomas Saine, "The Oasis of Happiness: Toward an Ontology of Play," *Yale French Studies*, no. 41 (1968): 19–30.

7. Julian Togelius, *Playing Smart: On Games, Intelligence, and Artificial Intelligence* (Cambridge, MA: MIT Press, 2019).

8. Mary L. Gray and Siddharth Suri, *Ghost Work: How to Stop Silicon Valley from Building a New Global Underclass* (Boston: Houghton Mifflin Harcourt, 2019).

9. Nick Srnicek, *Platform Capitalism* (Cambridge, UK: Polity Press, 2017).

10. Richard S. Sutton and Andrew G. Barto, *Reinforcement Learning: An Introduction*, 2nd ed. (Cambridge, MA: MIT Press, 2018); Noor Shaker, Julian Togelius, and Mark J. Nelson, *Procedural Content Generation in Games: A Textbook and an Overview of Current Research* (Basel: Springer, 2016).

11. Luis von Ahn et al., "CAPTCHA: Using Hard AI Problems for Security," in *Advances in Cryptology—EUROCRYPT 2003*, ed. Eli Biham (Berlin: Springer, 2003), 294–311.

12. https://artsexperiments.withgoogle.com/nonsense-laboratory/, February 1, 2022.

13. Mia Consalvo and Christopher A. Paul, *Real Games: What's Legitimate and What's Not in Contemporary Videogames* (Cambridge, MA: MIT Press, 2019).

14. Tim Ingold, "Toward an Ecology of Materials," *Annual Review of Anthropology* 41, no. 1 (2012): 427–442.

15. Ingold, 432.

16. Peter-Paul Verbeek, *What Things Do* (Pennsylvania: Pennsylvania State University Press, 2006).

17. Lucas D. Introna, "Towards a Post-Human Intra-Actional Account of Sociomaterial Agency (and Morality)," in *The Moral Status of Technical Artefacts*, ed. Peter Kroes and Peter-Paul Verbeek (Dordrecht: Springer Netherlands, 2014), 31–53.

18. Karen Barad, *Meeting the Universe Halfway: Quantum Physics and the Entanglement of Matter and Meaning* (Durham, NC: Duke University Press, 2007).

19. https://developer.apple.com/videos/play/wwdc2018/803/. February 1, 2022.

20. Wireless Lab, *FaceApp* (2016).

21. Consalvo and Paul, *Real Games.*

22. Kishonna L. Gray, *Race, Gender, and Deviance in Xbox Live: Theoretical Perspectives from the Virtual Margins* (London: Routledge, 2014); Adrienne Shaw, *Gaming at the Edge: Sexuality and Gender at the Margins of Gamer Culture* (Minneapolis: University of Minnesota Press, 2015).

23. Jean Baudrillard, *The System of Objects* (London: Verso, 2005), 114–119.

24. Susanna Paasonen, *Many Splendored Things: Thinking Sex and Play* (Cambridge, MA: MIT Press, 2018).

25. David Parisi, *Archaeologies of Touch* (Minneapolis: University of Minnesota Press, 2018).

Chapter 4

1. Thomas S. Henricks, *Play and the Human* Condition (Urbana: University of Illinois Press, 2016), 219.

2. Kendall L. Walton, *Mimesis As Make-Believe: On the Foundations of Representational Arts* (Cambridge, MA: Harvard University Press, 2007).

3. María Lugones, "Playfulness, 'World'-Travelling, and Loving Perception." *Hypatia* 2, no. 2 (1987), 15.

4. Sebastian Deterding, "The Game Frame: Systemizing a Goffmanian Approach to Video Game Theory," paper presented at "Breaking New Ground: Innovation in

Games, Play, Practice, and Theory," the 2009 Digital Games Research Association (DiGRA) conference, London, UK, September 1–4, 2009, http://www.digra.org/wp-content/uploads/digital-library/09287.43112.pdf.

5. Erving Goffman, *Encounters: Two Studies in the Sociology of Interaction* (Indianapolis: Bobbs-Merrill, 1961).

6. Ben Grosser, "What Do Metrics Want? How Quantification Prescribes Social Interaction on Facebook," *Computational Culture* 4 (2014), http://computationalculture.net/what-do-metrics-want/.

7. Gaby David and Carolina Cambre, "Screened Intimacies: Tinder and the Swipe Logic," *Social Media + Society* 2, no. 2 (2016): 1–11; Jacob Johanssen, "Gaming–Playing on Social Media," *Information, Communication and Society* 21, no. 9 (2018): 1204–1218; B. Garda Maria and Veli-Matti Karhulahti, "Let's Play Tinder! Aesthetics of a Dating App," *Games and Culture* 16, no. 2 (2021): 248–261.

8. Cardboard Computer, *Kentucky Route Zero* (Annapurna Interactive, 2011). Adam Robinson-Yu, *A Short Hike* (2019).

9. Grant Tavinor, *The Art of Videogames*. (Oxford: Wiley-Blackwell, 2009).

10. Frank Lantz et al., *Hey Robot* (2020).

11. Bernard Suits, *The Grasshopper: Games, Life and Utopia* (Toronto: University of Toronto Press, 1978).

12. C. Thi Nguyen, *Games: Agency as Art* (Oxford: Oxford University Press, 2020).

13. Alan Turing, "I—Computing Machinery and Intelligence," *Mind* 59, no. 236 (October 1, 1950): 433–460.

14. Joseph Weizenbaum, "ELIZA—a Computer Program for the Study of Natural Language Communication between Man and Machine," *Communications of the ACM* 9, no. 1 (January 1, 1966): 36–45.

15. For interesting takes on the famous Turing test, see Selmer Bringsjord, Paul Bello, and David Ferrucci, "Creativity, the Turing Test, and the (Better) Lovelace Test," in *The Turing Test*, ed. James H. Moor (Dordrecht: Springer Netherlands, 2003): 215–239; L. Floridi, "Turing's Three Philosophical Lessons and the Philosophy of Information," *Philosophical Transactions of the Royal Society A: Mathematical, Physical and Engineering Sciences* 370, no. 1971 (June 18, 2012): 3536–3542.

16. Joseph Weizenbaum, *Computer Power and Human Reason: From Judgment to Calculation* (San Francisco: Freeman, 1994).

17. Byron Reeves and Clifford Nass, *The Media Equation: How People Treat Computers, Television, and New Media Like Real People and Places*. (New York: Cambridge University Press, 1996).

18. A fascinating understanding of multiple agencies and care can be found in Maria Puig de la Bellacasa, "Matters of Care in Technoscience: Assembling Neglected Things," *Social Studies of Science* 41, no. 1 (December 7, 2010): 85–106.

19. Daniel Oberhaus, *Extraterrestrial Languages* (Cambridge, MA: MIT Press, 2019), 55.

20. Valerie Frissen et al., "Homo Ludens 2.0: Play, Media, and Identity." In *Playful Identities: The Ludification of Digital Media Cultures,* edited by Valerie Frissen, Sybille Lammes, Michiel de Lange, Jos de Mul, and Joost Raessens, 9–50 (Amsterdam: Amsterdam University Press, 2015).

21. Roger Caillois, *Man, Play and Games* (Urbana: University of Illinois Press, 2001).

22. Brian Sutton-Smith, *The Ambiguity of Play* (Cambridge, MA: Harvard University Press, 1997).

23. Julie E. Cohen, *Configuring the Networked Self.* (New Haven: Yale University Press, 2012).

24. Johanssen, "Gaming–Playing on Social Media," 1204–1218.

25. Betti Marenko and Philip van Allen, "Animistic Design: How to Reimagine Digital Interaction between the Human and the Nonhuman," *Digital Creativity* 27, no. 1 (April 26, 2016): 52–70.

26. Jin Huafeng and Wang Shuo, Voice-Based Determination of Physical And Emotional Characteristics of Users, US Patent 10096319B1, filed March 13, 2017, and issued October 9, 2018, https://patents.google.com/patent/US10096319B1/en.

27. Jessa Lingel and Kate Crawford, "'Alexa, Tell Me about Your Mother': The History of the Secretary and the End of Secrecy." *Catalyst: Feminism, Theory, Technoscience* 6, no. 1 (2020): 1–25.

28. Phil Turner and J. Tuomas Harviainen, eds., *Digital Make-Believe* (Basel: Springer International, 2016)

29. Natasha Dow Schüll, *Addiction by Design* (Princeton: Princeton University Press, 2014).

30. Ben Grosser, "What Do Metrics Want? How Quantification Prescribes Social Interaction on Facebook." *Computational Culture 4* (2014). http://computationalculture.net/what-do-metrics-want/

Chapter 5

1. Jay W. Forrester, "System Dynamics, Systems Thinking, and Soft OR," *System Dynamics Review* 10, no. 2–3 (1994): 245–256.

2. Donella H. Meadows, *Thinking in Systems: A Primer*, ed. Diana Wright (White River Junction, VT: Chelsea Green, 2009).

3. Whitney Phillips, *This Is Why We Can't Have Nice Things: Mapping the Relationship between Online Trolling and Mainstream Culture* (Cambridge, MA: MIT Press, 2015); Whitney Phillips, "The Oxygen of Amplification," *Data and Society* 22 (2018): 1–128; Whitney Phillips and Ryan M. Milner, *The Ambivalent Internet: Mischief, Oddity, and Antagonism Online* (London: Wiley, 2018).

4. Norbert Wiener, *The Human Use of Human Beings* (London: Free Association Books, 1989).

5. Wiener, 16, 18.

6. Wiener, 34.

7. Wiener, 31.

8. Wiener, 24.

9. Richard Schechner, "Playing," *Play and Culture* 1 (January 1, 1988): 3–19.

10. Sherry Turkle, *Life on the Screen* (New York: Simon & Schuster, 1997), and *The Second Self: Computers and the Human Spirit* (New York: Simon & Schuster, 1984); Julian Kücklich, "The Study of Computer Games as a Second-Order Cybernetic System," in *Computer Games and Digital Cultures Conference Proceedings*, edited by Frans Mäyrä, 101–111 (Tampere, Finland: Tampere University Press, 2002), http://www.digra.org/digital-library/publications/the-study-of-computer-games-as-a-second-order-cybernetic-system; Ted Friedman, "Civilization and Its Discontents: Simulation, Subjectivity, and Space," in *On a Silver Platter: CD-ROMs and the Promises of a New Technology*, ed. Greg M. Smity (New York: NYU Press, 1999), 132–150.

11. Alexander R. Galloway, *Gaming: Essays on Algorithmic Culture* (Minneapolis: University of Minnesota Press, 2006).

12. Stephanie Boluk and Patrick LeMieux, *Metagaming* (Minneapolis: University of Minnesota Press, 2017).

13. C. Thi Nguyen, *Games: Agency as Art* (Oxford: Oxford University Press, 2020).

14. Nintendo EAD and Nintendo EPD, *Animal Crossing* (Nintendo, 2001).

15. Ruha Benjamin, *Race after Technology* (Medford, MA: Polity Press, 2019).

16. Alexander Campolo and Kate Crawford, "Enchanted Determinism: Power without Responsibility in Artificial Intelligence," *Engaging Science, Technology, and Society* 6 (2020), https://estsjournal.org/index.php/ests/article/view/277.

17. David Sudnow, *Pilgrim in the Microworld* (New York: Warner Books, 1983).

18. Katie Salen and Eric Zimmerman, *Rules of Play: Game Design Fundamentals* (Cambridge, MA: MIT Press, 2003).

19. Ian Bogost, *Persuasive Games* (Cambridge, MA: MIT Press, 2007).

20. Robert Zubek, *Elements of Game Design* (Cambridge, MA: MIT Press, 2020).

21. Robin Hunicke, Marc Leblanc, and Robert Zubek, "MDA: A Formal Approach to Game Design and Game Research," *AAAI Workshop—Technical Report* 1 (2004).

22. Zubek, *Elements of Game Design*, 2

23. Zubek, 82.

24. Zubek, 82.

25. Miguel Sicart, "Against Procedurality," *Game Studies* 11, no. 3 (2011).

26. Zubek, *Elements of Game Design*, 1.

27. Meadows, *Thinking in Systems*, 2.

28. Meadows, 13.

29. Salen and Zimmerman, *Rules of Play*. chap. 18.

30. Paul N. Edwards, *The Closed World: Computers and the Politics of Discourse in Cold War America* (Cambridge, MA: MIT Press, 1996).

31. Edwards, 15.

32. Nick Dyer-Witheford and Greig De Peuter, *Games of Empire: Global Capitalism and Video Games* (Minneapolis: University of Minnesota Press, 2009).

33. Reed Berkowitz, "A Game Designer's Analysis Of QAnon," *Medium*, 2020, https://medium.com/curiouserinstitute/a-game-designers-analysis-of-qanon-580972548be5.

34. Dale Beran, *It Came from Something Awful* (New York: Macmillan, 2020); E. Gabriella Coleman, *Hacker, Hoaxer, Whistleblower, Spy: The Many Faces of Anonymous* (London: Verso Books, 2014); Nancy L. Rosenblum and Russell Muirhead, *A Lot of People Are Saying: The New Conspiracism and the Assault on Democracy* (Princeton: Princeton University Press, 2019); Joseph E. Uscinski, ed., *Conspiracy Theories and the People Who Believe Them* (Oxford: Oxford University Press, 2019).

35. Beran, *It Came from Something Awful*, 3–49.

36. C. Thi Nguyen, "Echo Chambers and Epistemic Bubbles," *Episteme* 17, no. 2 (2020): 141–161.

37. Miguel Angel Sicart (Vila), "The Banality of Simulated Evil: Designing Ethical Gameplay," *Ethics and Information Technology* 11, no. 3 (2009): 191–202.

38. David Graeber, "What's the Point If We Can't Have Fun?" Baffler, January 2014, 191, https://thebaffler.com/salvos/whats-the-point-if-we-cant-have-fun.

39. Bob Black, "Abolition of Work," 1985, https://theanarchistlibrary.org/library/bob-black-the-abolition-of-work/.

40. Wiener, *The Human Use of Human Beings*, 40.

41. Edwards, *The Closed World*, 15.

42. María Lugones, "Playfulness, 'World'-Travelling, and Loving Perception," *Hypatia* 2, no. 2 (1987): 15.

43. Lugones, 17.

44. Lugones, 16.

45. Lugones, 17.

46. Meadows, *Thinking in Systems*, 170.

Chapter 6

1. Mathias Fuchs, *Rereading Marx in the Age of Digital Capitalism* (London: Pluto Press, 2019).

2. Shoshana Zuboff, *The Age of Surveillance Capitalism: The Fight for a Human Future at the New Frontier of Power* (New York: Public Affairs, 2019).

3. Nick Dyer-Witheford and Greig De Peuter, *Games of Empire: Global Capitalism and Video Games* (Minneapolis: University of Minnesota Press, 2009); Emil L. Hammar et al., "Politics of Production: Videogames 10 Years after Games of Empire," *Games and Culture* 16, no. 3 (2019), 287–293.

4. Daniel Joseph, "The Discourse of Digital Dispossession: Paid Modifications and Community Crisis on Steam," *Games and Culture* 13, no. 7 (February 27, 2018): 690–707; Felan Parker, Jennifer R. Whitson, and Bart Simon, "Megabooth: The Cultural Intermediation of Indie Games," *New Media and Society* 20, no. 5 (June 5, 2017): 1953–1972.

5. Bernie DeKoven, *The Well-Played Game* (Cambridge, MA: MIT Press, 2013); Thomas Henricks, *Play and the Human Condition* (Urbana: University of Illinois Press, 2016).

6. Mark Fisher, *Capitalist Realism: Is There No Alternative?* (Winchester, UK: Zero Books, 2009).

7. Julian Kücklich, "FCJ-025 Precarious Playbour: Modders and the Digital Games Industry" (2005), http://five.fibreculturejournal.org/fcj-025-precarious-playbour-modders-and-the-digital-games-industry/.

8. Donna Haraway, "A Giant Bumptious Litter: Donna Haraway on Truth, Technology, and Resisting Extinction," *Logic Magazine*, December 7, 2019, https://logicmag.io/nature/a-giant-bumptious-litter/.

9. Phoebe Moore and Andrew Robinson, "The Quantified Self: What Counts in the Neoliberal Workplace," *New Media and Society* 18, no. 11 (September 17, 2015): 2774–2792; Chris Till, "Exercise as Labour: Quantified Self and the Transformation of Exercise into Labour," *Societies* 4, no. 3 (2014): 1–17.

10. Jean Piaget, *The Moral Judgement of the Child* (New York: Free Press, 1997).

11. Roger Caillois, *Man, Play and Games* (Urbana: University of Illinois Press, 2001).

12. Henricks, *Play and the Human Condition*, 51.

13. Johan Huizinga, *Homo Ludens* (Boston: Beacon Press, 1971).

14. Bill Gaver, "Designing for Homo Ludens, Still," in *(Re)Searching the Digital Bauhaus*, ed. Thomas Binder, Jonas Løwgren, and Lone Malmborg (London: Springer, 2009), 163–178.

15. Soraya Murray, *On Video Games: The Visual Politics of Race, Gender and Space* (London: Bloomsbury Academic, 2017).

16. C. Thi Nguyen, *Games: Agency as Art* (Oxford: Oxford University Press, 2020), 201.

17. Ian Bogost, "Why Gamification Is Bullshit," in *The Gameful World*, ed. Sebastian Deterding and Steffen P. Walz (Cambridge, MA: MIT Press, 2015), 65–80.

18. Virginia Eubanks, *Automating Inequality: How High-Tech Tools Profile, Police, and Punish the Poor* (New York: Picador, 2019).

19. Fuchs, *Rereading Marx in the Age of Digital Capitalism* (London: Pluto Press, 2019).

20. Galloway, *The Interface Effect* (New York: Polity Press, 2012).

21. Fisher, *Capitalist Realism.*

22. Fisher, 4.

23. Fisher, 21.

24. Fisher, 54.

25. Fisher, 14.

26. Fisher, 22.

27. Fisher, 79.

28. Nick Srnicek, *Platform Capitalism* (Cambridge, UK: Polity Press, 2017), 39.

29. Zuboff, *The Age of Surveillance Capitalism.*

30. Srnicek, *Platform Capitalism*, 92.

31. Srnicek, 41–42.

32. Srnicek, 46.

33. Fisher, *Capitalist Realism*, 42.

34. Nick Statt, "Amazon Expands Gamification Program That Encourages Warehouse Employees to Work Harder," *Verge*, March 15, 2021, https://www.theverge.com/2021/3/15/22331502/amazon-warehouse-gamification-program-expand-fc-games; James Vincent, "Amazon Turns Warehouse Tasks into Video Games to Make Work 'Fun,'" *Verge*, May 22, 2019, https://www.theverge.com/2019/5/22/18635272/amazon-warehouse-working-conditions-gamification-video-games.

35. At the time of editing this book, Amazon workers in New York successfully forced Amazon to recognize their union. Victories are still possible, and no enemy is too big against collective action.

36. Heike Geissler, *Seasonal Associate* (Los Angeles: Semiotext(e), 2018). A more academic account of the working conditions in Amazon warehouses can be found in Alessandro Delfanti, "Machinic Dispossession and Augmented Despotism: Digital Work in an Amazon Warehouse," *New Media and Society* 23, no. 1 (January 1, 2021): 39–55.

37. Donald F. Roy, "'Banana Time': Job Satisfaction and Informal Interaction," *Human Organization* 18, no. 4 (1959): 158–168.

38. Mary L. Gray and Siddharth Suri, *Ghost Work: How to Stop Silicon Valley from Building a New Global Underclass*. (Boston: Houghton Mifflin Harcourt, 2019), 122.

39. Gray and Suri, 5.

40. Hamid R. Ekbia and Bonnie A. Nardi, *Heteromation, and Other Stories of Computing and Capitalism* (Cambridge, MA.: MIT Press, 2017), 24–25, 14.

41. Ekbia and. Nardi, 24–25.

42. Ekbia and Nardi, 114.

43. Ekbia and Nardi, 49–50, 167–168.

44. "Quick, Draw! By Google Creative Lab: Experiments with Google," accessed April 6, 2021, https://experiments.withgoogle.com/quick-draw.

45. Alexander Campolo and Kate Crawford, "Enchanted Determinism: Power without Responsibility in Artificial Intelligence," *Engaging Science, Technology, and Society* 6 (January 8, 2020).

46. "Excavating AI," accessed April 6, 2021, https://excavating.ai; Cathy O'Neil, *Weapons of Math Destruction: How Big Data Increases Inequality and Threatens Democracy* (London: Penguin Books, 2017).

47. David B. Nieborg, "Apps of Empire: Global Capitalism and the App Economy," *Games and Culture* 16, no. 3 (May 2021): 305–316.

48. David Graeber, *The Utopia of Rules: On Technology, Stupidity, and the Secret Joys of Bureaucracy* (San Francisco: Melville House, 2016), 191.

49. Graeber, 193.

50. Richard Schechner, "Playing," *Play and Culture* 1 (January 1, 1988): 3–19.

51. Bob Black, "Abolition of Work" (1985), https://theanarchistlibrary.org/library/bob-black-the-abolition-of-work/; Holley Cantine, "Art: Play and Its Perversions," *Retort: A Quarterly Journal of Anarchism, Art and Reviews* (Fall 1947), https://theanarchistlibrary.org/library/holley-cantine-art-play-and-its-perversions; Alejandro de Acosta, "A Funny Thought on a New Way to Play," *AJODA* 26, no. 1 (2008), https://theanarchistlibrary.org/library/alejandro-de-acosta-a-funny-thought-on-a-new-way-to-play; G. Ogo and Drica Dejerk, "Soma: An Anarchist Play Therapy," *AJODA* 26, no. 2 (2008), https://theanarchistlibrary.org/library/ajoda-soma; Paul Z. Simons, "Seven Theses on Play," *Anarchy: A Journal of Desire Armed* 23 (1990): 11. https://archive.org/embed/ajoda-23.

52. María Lugones, "Playfulness, 'World'-Travelling, and Loving Perception" *Hypatia* 2, no. 2 (1987): 16

53. Donna Haraway, "A Giant Bumptious Litter: Donna Haraway on Truth, Technology, and Resisting Extinction," *Logic Magazine*, December 7, 2019, https://logicmag.io/nature/a-giant-bumptious-litter/.

Chapter 7

1. Philippa Foot, "The Problem of Abortion and the Doctrine of Double Effect," Oxford Review 5 (1967), 5–15.

2. Luciano Floridi, *The Ethics of Information* (Oxford: Oxford University Press, 2015).

3. David Graeber, "What's the Point If We Can't Have Fun?" *Baffler* no. 24 (January 2014).

Bibliography

Acosta, Alejandro de. "A Funny Thought on a New Way to Play." *AJODA* 26, no. 1 (2008). https://theanarchistlibrary.org/library/alejandro-de-acosta-a-funny-thought-on-a-new-way-to-play.

Ahn, Luis von, Manuel Blum, Nicholas J. Hopper, and John Langford. "CAPTCHA: Using Hard AI Problems for Security." In *Advances in Cryptology—EUROCRYPT 2003*, edited by Eli Biham, 294–311. Berlin: Springer, 2003.

Andersen, Christian Ulrik, and Pold Søren. *The Metainterface: The Art of Platforms, Cities, and Clouds*. Cambridge, MA: MIT Press, 2018.

Apperley, Thomas, and Darshana Jayemanne. "Game Studies' Material Turn." *Westminster Papers in Communication and Culture* 9, no. 1 (2012): 5–25.

Barad, Karen. *Meeting the Universe Halfway: Quantum Physics and the Entanglement of Matter and Meaning*. Durham, NC: Duke University Press, 2007.

Baudrillard, Jean. *The System of Objects*. London: Verso, 2005.

Bekker, Tilde, Janienke Sturm, and Berry Eggen. "Designing Playful Interactions for Social Interaction and Physical Play." *Personal and Ubiquitous Computing* 14, no. 5 (2009): 385–396.

Bellacasa, Maria Puig de la. "Matters of Care in Technoscience: Assembling Neglected Things." *Social Studies of Science* 41, no. 1 (2010): 85–106.

Benjamin, Ruha. *Race after Technology: Abolitionist Tools for the New Jim Code*. Medford, MA: Polity Press, 2019.

Beran, Dale. *It Came from Something Awful*. New York: All Points Books, 2019.

Berkowitz, Reed. "A Game Designer's Analysis of QAnon." *Medium*, January 30, 2020. https://medium.com/curiouserinstitute/a-game-designers-analysis-of-qanon-580972548be5.

Bethesda Game Studios. *Fallout 3*. Bethesda Softworks, 2008.

Black, Bob. "Abolition of Work." 1985. Retrieved January 30, 2022, from https://theanarchistlibrary.org/library/bob-black-the-abolition-of-work/.

Blizzard Entertainment. *World of Warcraft*. Blizzard Entertainment, 2004.

Bogost, Ian. *Persuasive Games*. Cambridge, MA: MIT Press, 2007.

Bogost, Ian. "Why Gamification Is Bullshit." In *The Gameful World*, edited by Sebastian Deterding and Steffen P. Walz, 65–80. Cambridge, MA: MIT Press, 2015.

Boluk, Stephanie, and Patrick LeMieux. *Metagaming: Playing, Competing, Spectating, Cheating, Trading, Making, and Breaking Videogames*. Minneapolis: University of Minnesota Press, 2017.

Braben, David, and Ian Bell. *Elite*. 1984.

Bringsjord, Selmer, Paul Bello, and David Ferrucci. "Creativity, the Turing Test, and the (Better) Lovelace Test." In *The Turing Test*, edited by James H. Moor, 215–239. Dordrecht: Springer, 2003.

Caillois, Roger. *Man, Play and Games*. Urbana: University of Illinois Press, 2001.

Campolo, Alexander, and Kate Crawford. "Enchanted Determinism: Power without Responsibility in Artificial Intelligence." *Engaging Science, Technology, and Society* 6 (2020).

Cantine, Holley. "Art: Play and Its Perversions." *Retort: A Quarterly Journal of Anarchism, Art and Reviews* (Fall 1947). https://theanarchistlibrary.org/library/holley-cantine-art-play-and-its-perversions.

Cardboard Computer. *Kentucky Route Zero*. Annapurna Interactive, 2011.

Certeau, Michel de, and Steven Rendall. *The Practice of Everyday Life*. Berkeley: University of California Press, 1984.

Coeckelbergh, Mark. *Moved by Machines: Performance Metaphors and Philosophy of Technology*. London: Routledge, 2019.

Cohen, Julie E. *Configuring the Networked Self*. New Haven, CT: Yale University Press, 2012.

Coleman, Gabriella. *Hacker, Hoaxer, Whistleblower, Spy: The Many Faces of Anonymous*. London: Verso Books, 2014.

ConcernedApe. *Stardew Valley*. 2016.

Consalvo, Mia. "There Is No Magic Circle." *Games and Culture* 4, no. 4 (2009): 408–417.

Consalvo, Mia, and Christopher A. Paul. *Real Games. What's Legitimate and What's Not in Contemporary Videogames*. Cambridge, MA: MIT Press, 2019.

Cook, Mike, S. Colton, J. Gow, and G. Smith. "General Analytical Techniques for Parameter-Based Procedural Content Generators." In *Proceedings of the 2019 IEEE Conference on Games*, 1–8. Piscataway, NJ: IEEE, 2019.

Cook, Mike, and Simon Colton. "Multi-Faceted Evolution of Simple Arcade Games." In *Proceedings of the 2011 IEEE Conference on Computational Intelligence and Games*, 289–296. Piscataway, NJ: IEEE, 2011.

Coole, Diana H., and Samantha Frost. *New Materialisms: Ontology, Agency, and Politics*. Durham: Duke University Press, 2010.

Couldry, Nick, and José van Dijck. "Researching Social Media as If the Social Mattered." *Social Media + Society* 1, no. 2 (2015): 1–7.

Crawford, Kate, and Vladan Joler. "Anatomy of an AI System." December 30, 2022. http://www.anatomyof.ai.

David, Gaby, and Carolina Cambre. "Screened Intimacies: Tinder and the Swipe Logic." *Social Media + Society* 2, no. 2 (2016): 1–11.

De la Bellacasa, Maria Puig. *Matters of Care*. Minneapolis: University of Minnesota Press, 2017.

DeKoven, Bernie. *The Well-Played Game*. Cambridge, MA: MIT Press, 2013.

DeLanda, Manuel. *A New Philosophy of Society: Assemblage Theory and Social Complexity*. London: Bloomsbury, 2019.

Delfanti, Alessandro. "Machinic Dispossession and Augmented Despotism: Digital Work in an Amazon Warehouse." *New Media and Society* 23, no. 1 (2021): 39–55.

Deterding, Sebastian. "Make-Believe in Gameful and Playful Design." In *Digital Make-Believe*, edited by Phil Turner and J. Tuomas Harviainen, 101–124. Basel: Springer International Publishing, 2016.

Deterding, Sebastian. "The Game Frame: Systemizing a Goffmanian Approach to Video Game Theory." Paper presented at "Breaking New Ground: Innovation in Games, Play, Practice, and Theory," the 2009 Digital Games Research Association (DiGRA) conference, London, UK, September 1–4, 2009. http://www.digra.org/wp-content/uploads/digital-library/09287.43112.pdf.

D'Ignazio, Catherine, and Lauren F. Klein. *Data Feminism*. Cambridge, MA: MIT Press, 2020.

Dippel, Anne, and Sonia Fizek. "Ludification of Culture." In *The Significance of Play and Games in Everyday Practices of the Digital Era*, edited by Gertraud Koch, 276–292. Abington: Routledge, 2017.

Dourish, Paul. "Seeing like an Interface." In *Proceedings of the 19th Australasian Conference on Computer-Human Interaction: Entertaining User Interfaces*, 1–8. New York: ACM, 2007.

Duncan, Margaret Carlisle. "Play Discourse and the Rhetorical Turn: A Semiological Analysis of Homo Ludens." *Play and Culture* 1 (1988): 28–42.

Dyer-Witheford, Nick, and Greig De Peuter. *Games of Empire: Global Capitalism and Video Games*. Minneapolis: University of Minnesota Press, 2009.

Edwards, Paul N. *The Closed World: Computers and the Politics of Discourse in Cold War America*. Cambridge, MA: MIT Press, 1996.

Ehrmann, Jacques, Cathy Lewis, and Phil Lewis. "Homo Ludens Revisited." *Yale French Studies*, no. 41 (1968): 31–57.

Ekbia, Hamid R., and Bonnie A. Nardi. *Heteromation, and Other Stories of Computing and Capitalism*. Cambridge, MA.: MIT Press, 2017.

Electronic Arts. *FIFA*. Electronic Arts, 1993.

Eubanks, Virginia. *Automating Inequality: How High-Tech Tools Profile, Police, and Punish the Poor*. New York: Picador, 2019.

Ferrara, John. *Playful Design: Creating Game Experiences in Everyday Interfaces*. New York: Rosenfeld Media, 2012.

Fink, Eugen, Ute Saine, and Thomas Saine. "The Oasis of Happiness: Toward an Ontology of Play." *Yale French Studies*, no. 41 (1968): 19–30.

Finn, Ed. *What Algorithms Want: Imagination in the Age of Computing*. Cambridge, MA: MIT Press, 2017.

Fisher, Mark. *Capitalist Realism: Is There No Alternative?* Winchester, UK: Zero Books, 2009.

Fizek, Sonia. "Automated State of Play: Rethinking Anthropocentric Rules of the Game." *Digital Culture and Society* 4, no. 1 (2018): 201–214.

Fizek, Sonia. "Interpassivity and the Joy of Delegated Play in Idle Games." *Transactions of the Digital Games Research Association* 3, no. 3 (April 30, 2018): 137–163.

Floridi, Luciano. *The Ethics of Information*. Oxford: Oxford University Press, 2015.

Floridi, Luciano. "Harmonising *Physis* and *Techne*: The Mediating Role of Philosophy." *Philosophy and Technology* 24 (2011): 1–3.

Floridi, Luciano. *The Philosophy of Information*. Oxford: Oxford University Press, 2013.

Floridi, Luciano. "Turing's Three Philosophical Lessons and the Philosophy of Information." *Philosophical Transactions of the Royal Society A: Mathematical, Physical and Engineering Sciences* 370, no. 1971 (2012): 3536–3542.

Flusser, Vilém. *Post-History*. Minneapolis: University of Minnesota Press, 2013.

Forrester, Jay W. "System Dynamics, Systems Thinking, and Soft OR." *System Dynamics Review* 10, no. 2–3 (1994): 245–256.

Frauenberger, Christopher. "Entanglement HCI The Next Wave?" *ACM Transactions on Human–Computer Interaction* 27, no. 1 (November 2019): 1–27.

Friedman, Ted. "Civilization and Its Discontents: Simulation, Subjectivity, and Space." In *On a Silver Platter: CD-ROMs and the Promises of a New Technology*, edited by Greg Smith, 132–150. New York: New York University Press, 1999.

Frissen, Valerie, Sybille Lammes, Michiel de Lange, Jos de Mul, and Joost Raessens. "Homo Ludens 2.0: Play, Media, and Identity." In *Playful Identities: The Ludification of Digital Media Cultures*, edited by Valerie Frissen, Sybille Lammes, Michiel de Lange, Jos de Mul, and Joost Raessens, 9–50. Amsterdam: Amsterdam University Press, 2015.

Fuchs, Mathias. *Rereading Marx in the Age of Digital Capitalism*. London: Pluto Press, 2019.

Gadamer, Hans Georg. *Truth and Method*. London: Continuum, 2004.

Galloway, A. *Uncomputable: Play and Politics in the Long Digital Age*. London: Verso Books, 2021.

Galloway, Alexander R. *Gaming: Essays on Algorithmic Culture*. Minneapolis: University of Minnesota Press, 2006.

Galloway, Alexander R. *The Interface Effect*. New York: Polity Press, 2012.

Garda, Maria B., and Veli-Matti Karhulahti. "Let's Play Tinder! Aesthetics of a Dating App." *Games and Culture* 16, no. 2 (March 2021): 248–261.

Gaver, Bill. "Designing for Homo Ludens, Still." In *(Re)Searching the Digital Bauhaus*, edited by Thomas Binder, Jonas Lowgren, and Lone Malmborg, 163–178. London: Springer, 2009.

Gehl, Robert W. "The Case for Alternative Social Media." *Social Media + Society* 1, no. 2 (September 22, 2015): 1–12.

Geissler, Heike. *Seasonal Associate*. Cambridge, MA: MIT Press, 2018.

Giddings, Seth. "A `'Pataphysics Engine." *Games and Culture* 2, no. 4 (October 1, 2007): 392–404.

Giddings, Seth. *Gameworlds: Virtual Media and Children's Everyday Play*. London: Bloomsbury, 2016.

Goffman, Erving. *Encounters: Two Studies in the Sociology of Interaction*. Indianapolis: Bobbs-Merrill, 1961.

Goffman, Erving. *Frame Analysis: An Essay on the Organization of Experience*. Cambridge, MA: Harvard University Press, 1974.

Gordon, Eric, and Gabriel Mugar. *Meaningful Inefficiencies: Civic Design in an Age of Digital Expediency*. Oxford: Oxford University Press, 2020.

Graeber, David. *The Utopia of Rules: On Technology, Stupidity, and the Secret Joys of Bureaucracy*. San Francisco: Melville House, 2016.

Graeber, David. "What's the Point If We Can't Have Fun?" *Baffler*, January 2014. https://thebaffler.com/salvos/whats-the-point-if-we-cant-have-fun.

Gray, Kishonna L. *Race, Gender, and Deviance in Xbox Live: Theoretical Perspectives from the Virtual Margins*. London: Routledge, 2014.

Gray, Mary L., and Siddharth Suri. *Ghost Work: How to Stop Silicon Valley from Building a New Global Underclass*. Boston: Houghton Mifflin Harcourt, 2019.

Grosser, Ben. "What Do Metrics Want? How Quantification Prescribes Social Interaction on Facebook." *Computational Culture* 4 (2014). http://computationalculture.net/what-do-metrics-want/.

Hammar, Emil L., Lars de Wildt, Souvik Mukherjee, and Caroline Pelletier. "Politics of Production: Videogames 10 Years after Games of Empire." *Games and Culture* 16, no. 3 (2019): 287–293.

Haraway, Donna. "A Giant Bumptious Litter: Donna Haraway on Truth, Technology, and Resisting Extinction." *Logic Magazine,* December 7, 2019. https://logicmag.io/nature/a-giant-bumptious-litter/.

Haraway, Donna. *Manifestly Haraway*. Minnesota: University of Minnesota Press, 2016.

Haraway, Donna. *Staying with the Trouble: Making Kin in the Chthulucene*. Durham: Duke University Press, 2016.

Hayles, N. Katherine. *My Mother Was a Computer: Digital Subjects and Literary Text*. Chicago: University of Chicago Press, 2005.

Heljakka, Katriina. "Contemporary Toys, Adults and Creative Material Culture: From Wow to Flow to Glow." In *Materiality and Popular Culture*, edited by Anna Malinowska and Karolina Lebek, 237–249. New York: Routledge, 2016.

Henricks, Thomas S. *Play and the Human Condition*. Urbana: University of Illinois Press, 2016.

Huafeng, Jin, and Wang Shuo. Voice-Based Determination of Physical and Emotional Characteristics of Users. US Patent 10096319B1, filed March 13, 2017, and issued October 9, 2018, https://patents.google.com/patent/US10096319B1/en.

Huizinga, Johan. *Homo Ludens: A Study of the Play-Element in Culture*. London: Beacon Press, 1971.

Humphreys, Lee. *The Qualified Self: Social Media and the Accounting of Everyday Life*. Cambridge, MA: MIT Press, 2018.

Hunicke, Robin, Marc Leblanc, and Robert Zubek. "MDA: A Formal Approach to Game Design and Game Research." *AAAI Workshop—Technical Report* 1 (2004).

Ingold, Tim. "Toward an Ecology of Materials.'" *Annual Review of Anthropology* 41, no. 1 (2012): 427–442.

Introna, Lucas D. "Towards a Post-Human Intra-Actional Account of Sociomaterial Agency (and Morality)." In *The Moral Status of Technical Artefacts*, edited by Peter Kroes and Peter-Paul Verbeek, 31–53. Dordrecht: Springer Netherlands, 2014.

Johanssen, Jacob. "Gaming-Playing on Social Media: Using the Psychoanalytic Concept of 'Playing' to Theorize User Labour on Facebook." *Information, Communication and Society* 21, no. 9 (September 2, 2018): 1204–1218.

Joseph, Daniel. "The Discourse of Digital Dispossession: Paid Modifications and Community Crisis on Steam." *Games and Culture* 13, no. 7 (February 27, 2018): 690–707.

Keogh, Brendan. *A Play of Bodies*. Cambridge, MA: MIT Press, 2018.

Kittler, Friedrich A. *Discourse Networks 1800/1900*. Stanford, CA: Stanford University Press, 2007.

Klevjer, Rune. "Enter the Avatar: The Phenomenology of Prosthetic Telepresence in Computer Games." In *The Philosophy of Computer Games*, edited by John Richard Sageng, Hallvard Fossheim, and Tarjei Mandt Larsen, 17–38. Dordrecht: Springer Netherlands, 2012.

Kücklich, Julian. "FCJ-025 Precarious Playbour: Modders and the Digital Games Industry," 2005. http://five.fibreculturejournal.org/fcj-025-precarious-playbour-modders-and-the-digital-games-industry/.

Kücklich, Julian. "The Study of Computer Games as a Second-Order Cybernetic System." In *Computer Games and Digital Cultures Conference Proceedings*, edited by Frans Mäyrä, 101–111. Tampere, Finland: Tampere University Press, 2002. http://www.digra.org/digital-library/publications/the-study-of-computer-games-as-a-second-order-cybernetic-system/.

Kunzelman, Cameron. "The Nonhuman Lives of Videogames." Georgia State University, 2014. https://scholarworks.gsu.edu/communication_theses/110/?fbclid=IwAR1PfJHw4adXD1TkmdVVzvUAMxYWp0_ZoZGLLXamuTRTR0HRY55oi3fbeAk.

Lantz, Frank, James Lantz, Hilary Lantz, and Mara Lantz. *Hey Robot*. 2020.

Latour, Bruno. *Reassembling the Social: An Introduction to Actor-Network-Theory*. Oxford: Oxford University Press, 2008.

Latour, Bruno. "Where Are the Missing Masses? The Sociology of a Few Mundane Artifacts." In *Shaping Technology/Building Society: Studies in Sociotechnical Change*, edited by Wiebe E. Bijker and John Law, 225–258. Cambridge, MA: MIT Press, 1992.

Laurel, Brenda. *Computers as Theatre*. 2nd ed. Boston, MA: Addison-Wesley, 1993.

Lefebvre, Henri, and John Moore. *Critique of Everyday Life: The One-Volume Edition*. London: Verso, 2014.

Lingel, Jessa, and Kate Crawford. "'Alexa, Tell Me about Your Mother': The History of the Secretary and the End of Secrecy." *Catalyst: Feminism, Theory, Technoscience* 6, no. 1 (2020): 1–25.

Lyotard, Jean-François. *The Postmodern Condition: A Report on Knowledge*. Minneapolis: University of Minnesota Press, 1984.

Lugones, María. "Playfulness, 'World'-Travelling, and Loving Perception." *Hypatia* 2, no. 2 (1987): 3–19.

Lupton, Deborah. *The Quantified Self*. New York: Polity Press, 2016.

Marenko, Betti, and Philip van Allen. "Animistic Design: How to Reimagine Digital Interaction between the Human and the Nonhuman." *Digital Creativity* 27, no. 1 (April 26, 2016): 52–70.

McKeown, Connor. "Playing with Materiality: An Agential-Realist Reading of SethBling's Super Mario World Code-Injection." *Information, Communication and Society* 21, no. 9 (2018): 1234–1245.

Meadows, Donella H. *Thinking in Systems: A Primer*. Edited by Diana Wright. White River Junction, VT: Chelsea Green, 2009.

Megacrit. *Slay the Spire*. Humble Bundle, 2019.

Meier, Sid. *Civilization*. MicroProse, 1991.

MIT Media Lab. "Moralmachine.Net," 2017. https://www.moralmachine.net.

Moore, Phoebe, and Andrew Robinson. "The Quantified Self: What Counts in the Neoliberal Workplace." *New Media and Society* 18, no. 11 (September 17, 2015): 2774–2792.

Murray, Janet Horowitz. *Hamlet on the Holodeck: The Future of Narrative in Cyberspace*. New York: Free Press, 1997.

Murray, Soraya. *On Video Games: The Visual Politics of Race, Gender and Space*. London: Bloomsbury Academic, 2017.

Nafus, Dawn, and Jamie Sherman. "Big Data, Big Questions: This One Does Not Go Up to 11: The Quantified Self Movement as an Alternative Big Data Practice." *International Journal of Communication* 8 (2014): 1784–1794.

Neff, Gina, and Dawn Nafus. *Self-Tracking*. Cambridge, MA: MIT Press, 2016.

Nguyen, C. Thi. "Echo Chambers and Epistemic Bubbles." *Episteme* 17, no. 2 (2020): 141–161.

Nguyen, C. Thi. *Games: Agency as Art*. Oxford: Oxford University Press, 2020.

Nieborg, David B. "Apps of Empire: Global Capitalism and the App Economy." *Games and Culture* 16, no. 3 (May 2021): 305–316.

Nintendo EAD, and Nintendo EPD. *Animal Crossing*. Nintendo, 2001.

Nippert-Eng, Christena. "Boundary Play." *Space and Culture* 8, no. 3 (August 1, 2005): 302–324.

Noble, Safiya Umoja. *Algorithms of Oppression: How Search Engines Reinforce Racism*. New York: NYU Press, 2018.

Oberhaus, Daniel. *Extraterrestrial Languages*. Cambridge, MA: MIT Press, 2019.

Ogo, G., and Drica Dejerk. "Soma: An Anarchist Play Therapy." *AJODA* 26, no. 2 (2008). https://theanarchistlibrary.org/library/ajoda-soma.

O'Neil, Cathy. *Weapons of Math Destruction: How Big Data Increases Inequality and Threatens Democracy*. London: Penguin Books, 2017.

Paasonen, Susanna. *Many Splendored Things: Thinking Sex and Play*. Cambridge, MA: MIT Press, 2018.

Paglen, Trevor. "Invisible Images: Your Pictures Are Looking at You." *Architectural Design* 89, no. 1 (2019): 22–27.

Parisi, David. *Archaeologies of Touch*. Minnesota: University of Minnesota Press, 2018.

Parker, Felan, Jennifer R Whitson, and Bart Simon. "Megabooth: The Cultural Intermediation of Indie Games." *New Media and Society* 20, no. 5 (June 5, 2017): 1953–1972.

Pasquale, Frank. *The Black Box Society: The Secret Algorithms That Control Money and Information*. Cambridge, MA: Harvard University Press, 2015.

Pearce, Celia. "Productive Play: Game Culture from the Bottom Up." *Games and Culture* 1, no. 1 (January 1, 2006): 17–24.

Phillips, Whitney. "The Oxygen of Amplification." *Data and Society* 22 (2018): 1–128.

Phillips, Whitney. *This Is Why We Can't Have Nice Things: Mapping the Relationship between Online Trolling and Mainstream Culture*. Cambridge, MA: MIT Press, 2015.

Phillips, Whitney, and Ryan M Milner. *The Ambivalent Internet: Mischief, Oddity, and Antagonism Online*. London: Wiley, 2018.

Piaget, Jean. *The Moral Judgement of the Child*. New York: Free Press, 1997.

Pichlmair, Martin, and Mads Johansen. "Designing Game Feel: A Survey." *IEEE Transactions on Games*, (2021), doi: 10.1109/TG.2021.3072241.

Poremba, Cindy. "Critical Potential on the Brink of the Magic Circle." Paper presented at "Situated Play," the 2007 Digital Games Research Association (DiGRA) conference, Tokyo, Japan, September 24–28, 2007. http://www.digra.org/wp-content/uploads/digital-library/07311.42117.pdf.

"Quick, Draw! By Google Creative Lab | Experiments with Google." Accessed January 30, 2022, https://experiments.withgoogle.com/quick-draw.

Reeves, Byron, and Clifford Nass. *The Media Equation: How People Treat Computers, Television, and New Media Like Real People and Places*. New York: Cambridge University Press, 1996.

Robinhood Markets. *Robinhood*. Robinhood Markets, 2015.

Robinson-Yu, Adam. *A Short Hike*. 2019.

Rosenberger, Robert. "The Importance of Generalized Bodily Habits for a Future World of Ubiquitous Computing." *AI and SOCIETY* 28, no. 3 (February 21, 2012): 289–296.

Rosenberger, Robert. "Multistability and the Agency of Mundane Artifacts: From Speed Bumps to Subway Benches." *Human Studies* 37, no. 3 (July 5, 2014): 369–392.

Rosenberger, Robert. "The Sudden Experience of the Computer." *AI and Society* 24, no. 2 (March 3, 2009): 173–180.

Rosenblum, Nancy L., and Russell Muirhead. *A Lot of People Are Saying: The New Conspiracism and the Assault on Democracy*. Princeton: Princeton University Press, 2019.

Roy, Donald F. "'Banana Time': Job Satisfaction and Informal Interaction." *Human Organization* 18, no. 4 (1959): 158–168.

Ruberg, Bonnie. *Video Games Have Always Been Queer*. New York: NYU Press, 2019.

Ruberg, Bonnie, and Adrienne Shaw. *Queer Game Studies*. Minneapolis: University of Minnesota Press, 2017.

Saker, Michael, and Leighton Evans. "Everyday Life and Locative Play: An Exploration of Foursquare and Playful Engagements with Space and Place." *Media, Culture and Society*, April 19, 2016, 1–15.

Salen, Katie, and Eric Zimmerman. *Rules of Play: Game Design Fundamentals*. Cambridge, MA: MIT Press, 2003.

Schechner, Richard. "Playing." *Play and Culture* 1 (January 1, 1988): 3–19.

Schüll, Natasha Dow. *Addiction by Design*. Princeton: Princeton University Press, 2014.

Seaver, Nick. "Knowing Algorithms." In *DigitalSTS: A Field Guide for Science and Technology Studies*, edited by Janet Vertesi and David Ribes, 412–422. Princeton: Princeton University Press, 2019.

Shaker, Noor, Julian Togelius, and Mark J. Nelson. *Procedural Content Generation in Games: A Textbook and an Overview of Current Research*. Berlin: Springer, 2016.

Sharon, Tamar. "Self-Tracking for Health and the Quantified Self: Re-Articulating Autonomy, Solidarity, and Authenticity in an Age of Personalized Healthcare." *Philosophy and Technology* 30, no. 1 (2017): 93–121.

Shaw, Adrienne. *Gaming at the Edge: Sexuality and Gender at the Margins of Gamer Culture*. Minneapolis: University of Minnesota Press, 2015.

Shklovski, Irina, Scott D. Mainwaring, Halla Hrund Skúladóttir, and Höskuldur Borgthorsson. "Leakiness and Creepiness in App Space: Perceptions of Privacy and Mobile App Use." In *Proceedings of the SIGCHI Conference on Human Factors in Computing Systems*, 2347–2356. New York: ACM, 2014.

Sicart, Miguel. "Against Procedurality." *Game Studies* 11, no. 3 (2011).

Sicart, Miguel. "The Banality of Simulated Evil: Designing Ethical Gameplay." *Ethics and Information Technology* 11, no. 3 (2009): 191–202.

Sicart, Miguel. "Defining Game Mechanics." *Game Studies* 8, no. 2 (2008).

Sicart, Miguel. *The Ethics of Computer Games*. Cambridge, MA: MIT Press, 2009.

Sicart, Miguel, and Irina Shklovski. "`Pataphysical Software: (Ridiculous) Technological Solutions for Imaginary Problems." In *Proceedings of the 2020 ACM Designing Interactive Systems Conference*, 1859–1771. New York: Association for Computing Machinery, 2020.

Simon, Bart. "Geek Chic." *Games and Culture* 2, no. 3 (2007): 175–193.

Simon, Bart. "Unserious." *Games and Culture* 12, no. 6 (2016): 605–618.

Simons, Paul Z. "Seven Theses on Play." *Anarchy: A Journal of Desire Armed* 23 (1990): 11. https://archive.org/embed/ajoda-23.

Slocombe, Will. "Playing Games with Technology:" *Osiris*, June 27, 2019.

Smith, Gillian. "Understanding Procedural Content Generation: A Design-Centric Analysis of the Role of PCG in Games." In *Proceedings of the SIGCHI Conference on Human Factors in Computing System*, 917–926. New York: Association for Computing Machinery, 2014.

Smith, Gillian. "What Do We Value in Procedural Content Generation?" In *Proceedings of the International Conference on the Foundations of Digital Games, FDG 2017*, 69:1–69:2.

Spiel, Katta, and Kathrin Gerling. "The Surrogate Body in Play." In *Proceedings of the Annual Symposium on Computer-Human Interaction in Play*, 397–411. New York: Association for Computing Machinery, 2019.

Srnicek, Nick. *Platform Capitalism*. Cambridge, UK: Polity Press, 2017.

Statt, Nick. "Amazon Expands Gamification Program That Encourages Warehouse Employees to Work Harder." *Verge*, March 15, 2021. https://www.theverge.com/2021/3/15/22331502/amazon-warehouse-gamification-program-expand-fc-games.

Stenros, Jaakko. "Playfulness, Play, and Games: A Constructionist Ludology Approach." PhD diss., Tampere University Press, 2015. http://tampub.uta.fi/handle/10024/96986. http://tampub.uta.fi/handle/10024/96986.

Subset Games. *Into the Breach*. Subset Games, 2018.

Suchman, Lucy. *Human–Machine Reconfigurations: Plans and Situated Actions*. Cambridge: Cambridge University Press, 2007.

Sudnow, David. *Pilgrim in the Microworld*. New York: Warner Books, 1983.

Suits, Bernard. *The Grasshopper: Games, Life and Utopia*. Toronto: University of Toronto Press, 1978.

Sullivan, Anne, Anastasia Salter, and Gillian Smith. "Games Crafters Play." In *Proceedings of the 13th International Conference on the Foundations of Digital Games*, 26:1–26:9. New York: Association of Computing Machinery, 2018. https://doi.org/10.1145/3235765.3235802.

Sutton, Richard S., and Andrew G. Barto. *Reinforcement Learning: An Introduction*, 2nd ed. Cambridge, MA: MIT Press, 2018.

Sutton-Smith, Brian. *The Ambiguity of Play*. Cambridge, MA: Harvard University Press, 1997.

Tavinor, Grant. *The Art of Videogames*. Oxford: Wiley-Blackwell, 2009.

Taylor, T. L. "The Assemblage of Play." *Games and Culture* 4, no. 4 (October 1, 2009): 331–339.

Till, Chris. "Exercise as Labour: Quantified Self and the Transformation of Exercise into Labour." *Societies* 4, no. 3 (2014): 1–17.

Togelius, Julian. *Playing Smart: On Games, Intelligence, and Artificial Intelligence*. Cambridge, MA: MIT Press, 2019.

Toy, Michael, Glenn Wichman, Ken Arnold, and Jon Lane. *Rogue*, 1980.

Trammell, Aaron. "Torture, Play, and the Black Experience." *GAME: The Italian Journal of Game Studies* 8, no. 9 (2020). https://www.gamejournal.it/torture-play/.

Turing, Alan. "I—Computing Machinery and Intelligence." *Mind* 59, no. 236 (October 1, 1950): 433–460.

Turkle, Sherry. *Life on the Screen: Identity in the Age of the Internet*. New York: Simon & Schuster, 1997.

Turkle, Sherry. *The Second Self: Computers and the Human Spirit*. New York: Simon & Schuster, 1984.

Turner, Phil, and J. Tuomas Harviainen, eds. *Digital Make-Believe*. Basel: Springer, 2016.

Uscinski, Joseph E., ed. *Conspiracy Theories and the People Who Believe Them*. Oxford: Oxford University Press, 2019.

Vallor, Shannon. "Flourishing on Facebook: Virtue Friendship and New Social Media." *Ethics and Information Technology* 14, no. 3 (January 8, 2011): 185–199.

Veale, Tony, and Michael Cook. *Twitterbots: Making Machines That Make Meaning*. Cambridge, MA: MIT Press, 2018.

Vectorpark. *Feed the Head*. IOS, 2007.

Verbeek, Peter-Paul. "Expanding Mediation Theory." *Foundations of Science* 17, no. 4 (October 8, 2011): 391–295.

Verbeek, Peter-Paul. *What Things Do*. State College: Pennsylvania State University Press, 2006.

Vertesi, Janet, and David Ribes. *DigitalSTS: A Field Guide for Science and Technology Studies*. Princeton: Princeton University Press, 2019.

Vincent, James. "Amazon Turns Warehouse Tasks into Video Games to Make Work 'Fun.'" *Verge*, May 22, 2019. https://www.theverge.com/2019/5/22/18635272/amazon-warehouse-working-conditions-gamification-video-games.

Walton, Kendall L. *Mimesis as Make-Believe: On the Foundations of Representational Arts*. Cambridge, MA: Harvard University Press, 2007.

Wardrip-Fruin, Noah. *Expressive Processing. Digital Fictions, Computer Games, and Software Studies*. Cambridge, MA: MIT Press, 2009.

Weizenbaum, Joseph. *Computer Power and Human Reason: From Judgment to Calculation*. San Francisco: Freeman, 1994.

Weizenbaum, Joseph. "ELIZA—a Computer Program for the Study of Natural Language Communication between Man and Machine." *Communications of the ACM* 9, no. 1 (1966): 36–45.

Whitson, Jennifer R. "Gaming the Quantified Self." *Surveillance and Society* 11, no. 1/2 (2013): 163–176.

Wiener, Norbert. *The Human Use of Human Beings*. London: Free Association Books, 1989.

Wilson, Douglas. "Designing for the Pleasures of Disputation-or- How to Make Friends by Trying to Kick Them!" PhD diss., IT University of Copenhagen, 2012. http://doougle.net/phd/Designing_for_the_Pleasures_of_Disputation.pdf.

Wireless Lab. *FaceApp*, 2016.

Woszczynski, Amy B., Philip L. Roth, and Albert H. Segars. "Exploring the Theoretical Foundations of Playfulness in Computer Interactions." *Computers in Human Behavior* 18, no. 4 (July 2002): 369–388.

Wyeth, Peta, Margot Brereton, Paul Roe, Ann Morrison, Yvonne Rogers, Alessandro Soro, and Daniel Johnson. "The Internet of Playful Things." In *Proceedings of the Annual Symposium on Computer-Human Interaction in Play*, 821–826. New York: Association for Computing Machinery, 2015.

Yu, Derek. *Spelunky*. Mossmouth LLC, 2008.

Zielinski, Siegfried, Peter Weibel, and Daniel Irrgang, eds. *Flusseriana. An Intellectual Toolbox*. Minneapolis: Univocal, 2015.

Zubek, Robert. *Elements of Game Design*. Cambridge, MA: MIT Press, 2020.

Zuboff, Shoshana. *The Age of Surveillance Capitalism: The Fight for a Human Future at the New Frontier of Power*. New York: Public Affairs, 2019.

Index

Note: Page numbers in *italics* denote figures.